U0518470

国际货代函电

主　编/范晓云　　肖　云
副主编/郭　伟　　韩冬艳　　陈中蕾
　　　　唐艳梅　　黄　丽

产教融合　　　校企合作

工学结合　　　知行合一

西南财经大学出版社

中国·成都

图书在版编目(CIP)数据

国际货代函电/范晓云,肖云主编;郭伟等副主编.—成都:西南财经
大学出版社,2023.7(2025.1重印)
ISBN 978-7-5504-5815-4

Ⅰ.①国… Ⅱ.①范…②肖…③郭… Ⅲ.①国际货运—货运
代理—英语—电报信函—写作 Ⅳ.①H315

中国国家版本馆 CIP 数据核字(2023)第 111660 号

国际货代函电

GUOJI HUODAI HANDIAN

主 编 范晓云 肖 云
副主编 郭 伟 韩冬艳 陈中蕾 唐艳梅 黄 丽

策划编辑:邓克虎
责任编辑:邓克虎
责任校对:乔 雷
封面设计:墨创文化 张姗姗
责任印制:朱曼丽

出版发行	西南财经大学出版社(四川省成都市光华村街 55 号)
网 址	http://cbs.swufe.edu.cn
电子邮件	bookcj@ swufe.edu.cn
邮政编码	610074
电 话	028-87353785
照 排	四川胜翔数码印务设计有限公司
印 刷	成都市火炬印务有限公司
成品尺寸	185 mm×260 mm
印 张	9.875
字 数	187 千字
版 次	2023 年 7 月第 1 版
印 次	2025 年 1 月第 2 次印刷
书 号	ISBN 978-7-5504-5815-4
定 价	35.00 元

前言

国际货代函电是高职院校国际商务专业的一门专业核心课程。本教材的编写旨在培养学生翻译和写作英语函电的技能，使学生具备独立运用英语处理进出口货物代理往来业务的能力，并适应社会对外贸应用型和技能型人才的需求，从而使学生能顺利走上工作岗位。

本教材围绕进出口外贸业务编写，内容包括国际货运代理（international freight forwarding agent），询盘与报盘（inquiry and offer），确认信息（confirmation），还盘（counter-offer），信息变更（information change），达成协议（acceptance），投诉、索赔和理赔（complaint，claim and settlement）等环节中的国际商务英语信函的撰写。全书包含七个学习任务模块，每个任务设置了工作情境描述、多个学习活动、信函写作技巧、典型范例、操作练习、信函常用表达方式等环节。

本教材具有实践性强、可操作性强的特点，采用以外贸工作人员的工作流程为主线并结合案例分析的模式，以一体化课程改革的要求构建教材框架，体现项目教学、任务驱动、工学结合的项目教材编写模式，凸显"以应用为目的，以必需、够用为度"的原则，有利于培养学生成为应用型、复合型、外向型的外贸业务人才。

本教材所有参编人员均来自教学一线，有着多年的国际贸易物流经验和技工院校实践教学经验。教材由范晓云担任主编，郭伟、韩冬艳、肖云担任主审，陈中蕾、唐艳梅、黄丽等教师参与编写。本教材由深圳鹏城技师学院资助出版。

由于编者的水平和经验有限，书中不足之处在所难免，竭诚希望得到读者批评指正。

编者

2023 年 3 月

目录

MULU

学习任务一　国际货运代理认知

工作情境描述

　　Joey 是某高校国际贸易专业刚毕业的学生，应聘担任深圳某货运代理公司国际货代员。刚进公司，经理安排 Joey 进行为期两周的企业培训，他认为这是浪费时间，没有必要。

学习任务解析

　　学习任务见图 1-1。

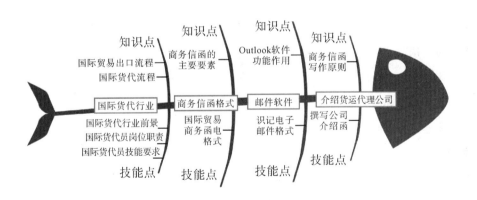

图 1-1　学习任务

建议课时

　　8 课时

工作流程与活动

学习活动 1　国际货代行业认知

学习活动 2　商务信函格式认知

学习活动 3　商务信函软件认知

学习活动 4　介绍货运代理公司

学习活动 1　国际货代行业认知

学习目标

1. **知识目标**

◆能熟记国际贸易出口流程。

◆能阐述国际货代流程。

2. **技能目标**

◆能分享国际货代行业前景。

◆能描述国际货代员的技能要求。

3. **素养目标**

◆通过个人展示或小组合作增强沟通表达能力。

◆通过专业知识的学习增强工作岗位的认知。

4. **思政目标**

◆通过中国加入世界贸易组织的事件，增强学生的民族自豪感。

◆通过中国加入世界贸易组织的事件，加强中国对外开放基本国策的学习。

学习课时

4 课时

学习过程

WTO 知多少？

世界贸易组织（World Trade Organization，WTO），简称世贸组织，是一个独立于联合国的永久性国际组织，总部位于瑞士日内瓦。

世界贸易组织的目标是建立一个完整的，包括货物、服务、与贸易有关的投资及知识产权等更具活力、更持久的多边贸易体系。

2001 年 12 月 11 日，中国正式加入世界贸易组织，成为第 143 个成员。

一、国际贸易出口流程回顾

【任务要求】请将以下的词组按照出口流程的顺序进行排序，并填写在下面空白处。

核销退税、运输、租船订舱、集港报关、报检备货、制单结汇、拣货出库、签订贸易合同

_____

_____

二、国际货代行业

【任务要求】请认真阅读以下段落，学习国际货物运输代理业的概念，并做好课堂学习笔记。

International cargo forwarding businesses are those enterprises which accept the entrustment of consignors, consignees and carriers to conduct international cargo transportation and related business on their behalf, and then charge service fees accordingly. Their major tasks include: arranging customs clearance, delivery, storage, dispatching, inspection, packing, and transferring of the cargo, shipping space booking, etc.

_____

_____

_____

_____

_____

三、国际货代员技能要求

【任务要求】请结合教材，利用网络、软件，了解国际货代行业的前景，观看微视频，复述国际货代员的技能要求，并填写在下面空白处。

_____

_____

_____

_____

四、请思考国际货代流程

【任务要求】以小组为单位进行讨论学习，5 分钟后展示学习成果，进行总结归纳后每人独立填写工作页内容。

_____

_____

_____

_____

_____

_____

学习活动 2　商务信函格式认知

学习目标

1. **知识目标**
   - ◆能识记商务信函的主要要素。
   - ◆能熟练掌握商务信函全齐头式。
2. **技能目标**
   - ◆能描述商务信函的主要要素。
   - ◆能识记国际贸易商务函电格式。

3. 素养目标

◆通过个人展示或小组合作增强沟通表达能力。

◆通过专业知识的学习增强工作岗位的认知。

学习课时

1 课时

学习准备

A3 空白纸、马克笔、磁铁

学习过程

一、商务信函的主要要素

【任务要求】请仔细观察邮件内容，用英文描述商务信函的主要要素。

_____

_____

_____

_____

_____

_____

_____

二、商务信函格式

商务信函有多种格式，较常用的有以下三种：缩进式（indented style）、全齐头式（full block style）和混合式（modified block style）。写信人可根据需要和个人喜好进行选择。

【任务要求】请仔细观察邮件格式（见图 1-2、图 1-3、图 1-4），总结归纳三大基本格式中的要点。

China National Linght Industrial Products
Imp.&Exp.Co
82 Dong An Men Street,Beijing,China
Tel:010-3366666   E-mail:dog@163.com
Fax:010-555567   Post Code:2345
May,2009

Our Ref.No:JVD/HZ
Mr.LiMing
Sales Manager
Mid-West Imp.&Exp. Co
12 East Tenth Street
Chicago,Illinois60687,USA
                    Attention:Import Department
Dear Sirs,

                    Chinese Color TV Sets
    Thank you for your inquiry of Oct.10 about our Color TV Sets.Here we enclose our catalogues and price list for
your reference.
    In case of your requiring further information,please fax us.We look forward to hearing from you soon.

                    Yours sincerely
        China National Linght Industrial Products
                    Imp.&Exp

                    (hand-signed)
                    Jiang Dawei

Letterhead (信头)

Reference NO. （参考号、发文编号）   Date （日期）

Inside name and address （信内地址）

Salutation （称呼）

                    Subject Line （主题）

Body of the letter （正文）

                    Complimentary Close （结束敬语）

                    Signature （签名）

Enclosure Notation （附件）

Carbon Copy Notation （抄送）

Postcript （附言、注）

图 1-2   商务信函邮件一

_____

_____

_____

_____

China National Linght Industrial Products Imp.&Exp.Co
82 Dong An Men Street,Beijing,China

Tel:010-3366666　　E-mail:dog@163.com
Fax:010-555567　　Post Code:2345
6 May,2009
Our Ref.No:JVD/HZ
Mr.LiMing
Sales Manager
Mid-West Imp.&Exp. Co
12 East Tenth Street
Chicago,Illinois60687,USA
Attention:Import Department
Dear Sirs,
Chinese Color TV Sets
Thank you for your inquiry of Oct.10 about our Color TV Sets.Here we enclose our catalogues and price list for your reference.
In case of your requiring further information,please fax us.We look forward to hearing from you soon.

Yours sincerely
China National Linght Industrial Products Imp.&Exp.Co
　(hand-signed)
Jiang Dawei

　WY/ML
Encls:A . Catalogues
B.　Price
CC:London Branch

P.S.Some other information will be send to you later

Letterhead (信头)

Reference NO.（参考号、发文编号）

Date（日期）

Inside name and address （信内地址）

Salutation （称呼）

Subject Line（主题）

Body of the letter （正文）

Complimentary Close （结束敬语）

Signature （签名）

Enclosure Notation（附件）

Carbon Copy Notation（抄送）

Postcript（附言、注）

图 1-3　商务信函邮件二

China National Linght Industrial Products Imp.&Exp.Co
82 Dong An Men Street,Beijing,China

Tel:010-3366666   E-mail:dog@163.com
Fax:010-555567   Post Code:2345
                              6 May,2009

Our Ref.No:JVD/HZ
Mr.LiMing
Sales Manager
Mid-West Imp.&Exp. Co
12 East Tenth Street
Chicago,Illinois60687,USA

Attention:Import Department

Dear Sirs,

Chinese Color TV Sets

Thank you for your inquiry of Oct.10 about our Color TV Sets.Here we enclose our catalogues and price list for your reference.

In case of your requiring further information,please fax us.We look forward to hearing from you soon.

Yours sincerely
China National Linght Industrial Products Imp.&Exp.Co
(hand-signed)
Jiang Dawei

WY/ML
Encls:A . Catalogues
          B. Price List
CC:London Branch

P.S.Some other information will be send to you later

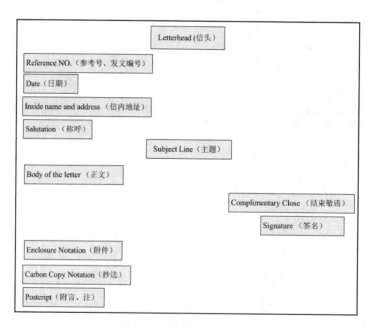

图 1-4   商务信函邮件三

知识链接

1. 信头（letterhead）

信头包括公司名称、地址、电话、传真、电子邮箱等内容，每个信息不可相互连接。其位置在页首居中。

2. 日期（date）

日期位于信头下一行，位置靠左或靠右皆可，日期不可缩写，通常有以下两种方式：12th March，2011（英式）；March 12，2011（美式）。

3. 参考号/发文编号（reference No.）

参考号/发文编号用于对信函进行编号，便于分类归档和日后查询，一般打印在日期上面或下面。参考号无固定格式，可选择最方便自身归档查询的方式表示。

4. 信内地址（inside name and address）

信内地址位于正文左上方，日期下面空一行处，内容包括收信人的名称和地址，若信是写给公司的，则只需写上公司的名称和地址；若写信人希望将此信交给某一特定的人，可在该人的名字前面加上"attention"字样。

5. 称呼（salutation）

称呼是写信人对收信人的尊称，一般位于收信人地址下面空一行处，通常是从左边顶格写起，在后面加上逗号或冒号。多以"Dear"开头，Dear Mr./Ms./Miss；Dear Sirs；若是写给某个公司而不知道收信人姓名的，则一般采用 Dear Sirs/Gentlemen。

6. 主题（subject line）

商务信函习惯在信的正文上方使用一个标题，以便收信人立即知道信件的主旨，也有利于归档查询。主题可用加底线或加粗字体以示突出，其位置居左或居中均可，常以 Subject 或 Re 做引导词，也可不用。

7. 正文（body of the letter）

正文是商务信函的主体，用来清楚、简明地概括写信人的观点、意见、愿望和要求等。较长的信可分成若干段落，每一个主题独立成段。各个段落之内常用单倍行距，段落之间常用双倍行距。

8. 结束敬语（complimentary close）

结束敬语与称呼对应，是表示写信人对收信人的一种谦称，使信函较礼貌地结束，而不至于让收信人感觉突然从正文跳到结尾。结束敬语位置在正文之后一至两行之外，从正

文偏右写或从左边顶格写，只需第一个单词的首字母大写，后面加上逗号。

9. 签名（signature）

签名是商务信函中极为重要的部分，因为签名具有法律效力。签名者对信中所述的内容承担一定的责任，因此，签名要清晰可辨，独具风格。签名部分除了要打印写信人名字及职务外，还需要写信人亲笔签名。为了表明性别，可以在签名时手写或打印 Mr. /Ms. 等字样。

10. 附件（enclosure notation）

如果信件中还有附件，则应在信的下方注明 Enc（s）. 或 Encl.。

11. 抄送（carbon copy notation）

如果信函还应抄送给除收信人外的其他人，常用 CC（carbon copy）表示，写在附件下方。

12. 附言/注（postscript, P.S.）

当写信人在信中忘了某事而需要补充的时候，可在 P.S. 后面加上想补充的内容，放在信的最后。在现代信函中，附言的作用已不局限于提及某件被遗忘的事，而是作为强调某件事的一种手段，以引起对方注意。

学习拓展

（　）1. letterhead　　　　　a. 事由

（　）2. reference　　　　　b. 附言

（　）3. body　　　　　　　c. 签字

（　）4. salutation　　　　　d. 文档号

（　）5. subject line　　　　e. 信头

（　）6. signature　　　　　f. 称呼

（　）7. postscript　　　　　g. 正文

学习活动3　商务信函软件认知

学习目标

1. 知识目标

　◆能理解 Outlook 软件的功能作用。

　◆能识记电子邮件格式。

2. 技能目标

　◆能熟练操作 Outlook 软件。

3. 素养目标

　◆通过专业软件的学习提升工作岗位的技能。

学习课时

1 课时

学习准备

Outlook 软件

学习过程

一、Outlook 软件的功能作用

Outlook 不是电子邮箱的提供者，它是 Windows 操作系统的一个收、发、写、管理电子邮件的自带软件，就像 Foxmail 一样，是一个工具，而不是邮箱。我们可以利用这个工具把邮箱账号加载到其中，不用登录网页邮箱，只利用 Outlook 就可以随时收发邮件了，并且所有的收发邮件都会在本地硬盘中保存一份，可以随时查看。

二、电子邮件格式

【任务要求】请查阅邮件内容（见图1-5），翻译商务信函电子邮件各主要要素。

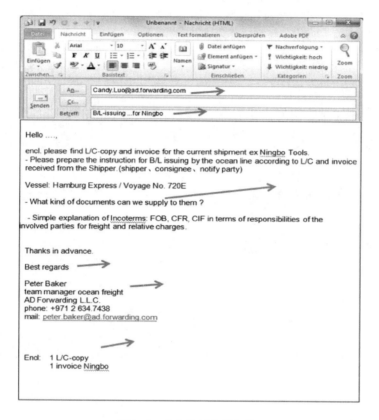

图1-5　商务信函电子邮件

学习活动 4　介绍货运代理公司

学习目标

1. 知识目标

◆能理解商务信函的写作原则。

◆能识记简单英文句式的构成。

2. 技能目标

◆能使用英文撰写简单句式。

◆能运用英文简单介绍货运代理公司。

3. 素养目标

◆通过小组讨论和角色扮演，提升工作岗位认知。

◆通过专业知识的学习，增强工作岗位技能。

学习课时

2 课时

学习准备

Outlook 软件

学习过程

一、商务信函写作原则

☐ completeness _____

☐ concreteness _____

☐ clearness _____

☐ conciseness _____

☐ courtesy _____

☐ consideration _____

☐ correctness _____

二、函电中的语言特点

【任务要求】请复述函电中的语言特点。

_____

_____

国际货代函电
GUOJI HUODAI HANDIAN

_____

_____

_____

_____

_____

_____

_____

三、撰写邮件

【任务要求】请根据以下商业信息给 cindyfan@pc.com 发送一份公司介绍的邮件。

深圳市××物流有限公司成立于 2022 年 12 月，经营范围包括货运代理（不含限制项目）、初级农产品的销售及国内贸易（不含专营等）。

深圳市××物流有限公司是一家第三方跨境生鲜冷链服务企业，主要事业版块包括生鲜跨境通平台、冷链运输平台、冷链枢纽港平台、供应链金融平台；专业承接跨境生鲜产品（水果、肉类、水产品、奶制品等冷冻冷藏食品），企业非核心业务外包。

公司致力构建以信息流、商流、资金流、物流为载体，以代理通关、代理冷链运输、代理接驳中转、代垫资金为核心的跨境生鲜整合型冷链服务平台。

【任务分析】

_____

_____

_____

_____

【制订方案】

_____

_____

_____

_____

_____

_____

_____

【任务实施】

_____

_____

_____

_____

_____

_____

_____

_____

_____

_____

_____

_____

_____

_____

_____

_____

_____

学习任务一（1）　英文词汇学习

学习任务二 询盘与报盘

工作情境描述

Joey 在深圳某货运代理公司完成为期两周的企业培训后，经理要求其在部门岗位间轮岗一个月，现从业务员岗位开始做起。运营部门下达开发海外市场的工作任务，希望在目标市场能发展 1~2 个客户。

学习任务解析

学习任务见图 2-1。

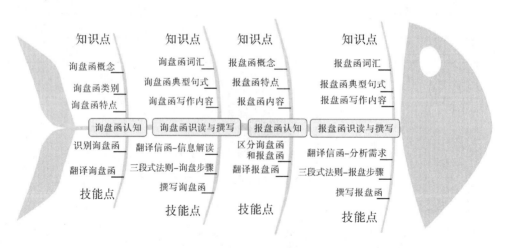

图 2-1 学习任务

建议课时

16 课时

工作流程与活动

学习活动 1　询盘函认知

学习活动 2　询盘函识读与撰写

学习活动 3　报盘函认知

学习活动 4　报盘函识读与撰写

学习活动 1　询盘函认知

学习目标

1. **知识目标**

◆能充分理解询盘函的概念。

◆能识记询盘函的类别。

◆能了解询盘函的特点。

2. **技能目标**

◆能识记询盘函的概念。

◆能复述询盘函的类别。

◆能识别询盘函。

3. **素养目标**

◆通过多样化学习方式提高自主学习能力，增强英语学习兴趣。

◆通过小组合作增强沟通表达能力，提高与国际客户沟通交流的信心。

4. **思政目标**

◆通过询盘函发信主体，强调中国国际地位的不断提升，增强民族自豪感。

学习课时

2 课时

学习过程

　　随着经济全球化深入发展，世界各国经济联系日益紧密，国际贸易规模不断扩大。2022 年，我国进出口总值突破 40 万亿元，达到 42.07 万亿元（同比增长 7.7%），其中：出口额为 23.97 万亿元（同比增长 10.5%），进口额为 18.1 万亿元（同比增长 4.3%）。我国连续 6 年保持世界第一货物贸易国地位。

一、询盘函概念与类别

　　【任务要求】请根据知识链接内容，将询盘函相关知识提炼并填制在图 2-2 中。

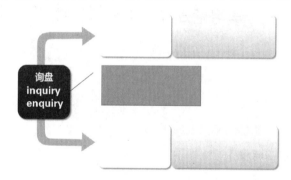

图 2-2　询盘函相关知识

知识链接

　　1. enquiry（询价或询盘）

　　询价或询盘是一种询问，是买方向卖方就某项商品交易条件提出询问的信函。询价的目的是请对方报出商品价格，对商品质量、交付期、支付方式等提出询问。询价对交易双方都没有法律上的约束力，其分为一般询盘和具体询盘。一般询盘（general enquiry），是买方为了了解情况向卖主索取商品目录、价目单、样品等。具体询盘（specific enquiry），是买方有做买卖的要求，指定商品要求卖主报盘。

　　2. quotation（报价）

　　报价是指在国际或国内贸易中，买方向卖方询问商品价格，卖方通过考虑自己产品的成本、利润、市场竞争力等因素，报出可行的价格。

学习任务二（1） 询盘认知 英文词汇学习

二、识别询盘函

【任务要求】请借助网络工具阅读以下信函，并翻译询盘函。

Sample Letter 1

Dear Mr. Liu,

We are impressed by lady's leather bags that were displayed in your exhibition hall at the 16th China Yiwu International Commodities Fair that was held in Yiwu City from Oct. 21 to Oct. 25, 2010.

We are a leading importer of leather bags that enjoys a high reputation in America. At present, we are looking for a manufacturer who could supply us with a wide range of lady's leather bags. We would be very grateful if you would send us your latest catalogue and price list.

We are looking forward to your early reply.

Yours faithfully,

Tony Parker

Sample Letter 2

Dear Mr. Parker,

We warmly welcome your inquiry of November 15 and thank you for your interest in our lady's leather bags.

We are enclosing our latest illustrated catalogue and price list you ask for. We feel confident that you will find the goods are both superior in quality and very reasonable in price. We allow a proper discount according to the quantity ordered. As for the payment terms we usually require confirmed, irrevocable Letter of Credit payable by draft at sight.

If you would like further information, please call me or send e-mail to me and we shall do our best to your request.

Your early reply is highly appreciated.

Yours sincerely,

Liu Qiang

【任务分析】请阅读信函，小组讨论并回答以下问题。

1. Which letter is enquiry? Sample letter one or sample letter two?

_____

2. What are the characteristics of an enquiry letter? Which sentence can help you to make a decision?

_____

_____

_____

3. What is the main idea of each paragraph? (reply in Chinese)

_____

_____

【制订方案】请小组讨论，并根据商务信函三段式法则拟出以上询盘函语法知识点。

_____

_____

_____

_____

【任务实施】请采用专业角度翻译询盘函。

_____

_____

_____

_____

_____

_____

学习活动 2　询盘函识读与撰写

学习目标

1. 知识目标

◆能熟记国际货代询盘业务中涉及的专业术语。

◆能充分理解询盘函的写作内容。

◆能熟记询盘函的基本词汇。

2. 技能目标

◆能熟练掌握商务信函三段式法则。

◆能熟练使用电脑，熟悉常用操作软件。

◆能认识并准确运用各种贸易术语和条款。

◆能识别函电中的特殊用语，根据中心词汇准确把握函电意图。

◆能够根据客户要求，运用英语灵活处理询盘函中的日常业务。

3. 素养目标

◆通过情景模拟增强对工作岗位的认知感。

◆通过角色扮演及业务分析，提升工作岗位应变能力。

◆通过多样化学习方式提高自主学习能力，增强英语学习兴趣。

◆通过小组合作增强沟通表达能力，提高与国际客户沟通交流的信心。

4. 思政目标

◆通过邮件内容识别各个国家的港口，认识"一带一路"沿线城市。

学习课时

6 课时

学习过程

"一带一路"（the Belt and Road，缩写 B&R）是"丝绸之路经济带"和"21世纪海上丝绸之路"的简称，2013年9月和10月由中国国家主席习近平分别提出建设"新丝绸之路经济带"和"21世纪海上丝绸之路"的合作倡议。依靠中国与有关国家既有的双多边机制，借助既有的、行之有效的区域合作平台，"一带一路"旨在借用古代丝绸之路的历史符号，高举和平发展的旗帜，积极发展与沿线国家的经济合作伙伴关系，共同打造政治互信、经济融合、文化包容的利益共同体、命运共同体和责任共同体。

截至2022年12月7日，中国已与150个国家、32个国际组织签署200余份共建"一带一路"合作文件。

一、识读询盘函

From：John Binh-Cargo Connection（Vietnam）
Sent：2021-09-09 10：47：09
To：Jennifer Ye；antonychen@ cc-cargo connection. com；
Subject：FCL inquiry：Jiangmen to Oklahoma，USA

Dear Jennifer,
Shipper：Kaiping City Scaler Building Material Company Limited
Xinhua RD, Xinchang, Kaiping City, Guangdong, China 529300
Consignee：Red Star Glass Tile Company
7762-A N. Owasso Expy Owasso，OK 74055
Purchase Order：S090312
Commodity：Glass tile ＝Mosaic （2 344. 70m^2）
Price Terms：FOB Jiangmen
The goods will be ready within 3 weeks from now
Could you please check and advise all costs from Jiangmen port to
Los Angeles port
Oklahoma terminal
We are looking forward to hearing from you.
Best regards,
John

Useful Notes：

1. shipper（发货人）

2. consignee（收货人）

3. volume（体积；平台；容量）

4. pallet（托盘；平台；运货板）

5. terminal（航空站；终点站）

6. terms［（协议、合同的）条件，条款］

7. advise（通知；正式告知）

　　e. g. Please advise us of any change in your plan. 你们的计划若有变更请告诉我们。

8. FCL＝full container load（整箱货，拼箱货的相对用语）

拓展知识：

　　所有的拼箱货物最终都要拼成一个整箱运出去。通常情况下，由一个或者几个发货人出运一批货物，通过货代向船运公司订一个整箱，到达目的港，收货人直接提货自行处理货物，最后把箱子还回去。相关术语有：

（1）整箱交、整箱接（FCL/FCL）；

（2）拼箱交、拆箱接（LCL/LCL）；

（3）整箱交、拆箱接（FCL/LCL）；

（4）拼箱交、整箱接（LCL/FCL）。

9. expy＝expressway（高速公路）

10. purchase order（采购单；订单）

11. glass tile（玻璃砖）

12. 1×20dc［一个 20 英尺（1 英尺＝0.304 8 米，下同）标准小柜子］

拓展知识：

　　DC＝dry container［干货柜，干货集装箱，专门用于装干货（dry cargo），与之相对应的是冷藏集装箱（reefer container）］

13. FOB＝free on board（… named port of shipment）［船上交货价格（离港价格），习惯称为装运港船上交货］

拓展知识：

　　按 FOB 成交，由买方负责派船接运货物，买方应在合同规定的装运港和规定的期限内，将货物装上买方指定的船只，并及时通知买方。货物在装船时越过船舷，风险及由卖方转移至买方。

14. OK＝Oklahoma （俄克拉荷马州）

15. Hochiminh City （胡志明市）

16. Vietnam （越南）

17. executive director （执行董事）

【任务分析】请认真阅读以上信函，回答以下问题。

1. Where is the letter from?

2. Where is the freight from and to?

3. What does John want from Jennifer?

4. When will the goods be ready?

【任务分析】请根据信函完成下列信息空白处的填写。

Jennifer receives a letter from John, the ＿＿＿＿＿＿＿＿＿＿＿＿＿ of v－mart （logistics） CO., LTD. He inquires about ＿＿＿＿＿＿＿ from Jiangmen port to ＿＿＿＿＿ ＿＿＿＿＿＿＿＿＿＿＿＿＿. He provides some detailed information：the shipper, ＿＿＿＿＿＿＿＿, purchase order, ＿＿＿＿＿＿＿＿, volume, ＿＿＿＿＿＿＿＿, and ＿＿＿＿＿＿＿ etc.

【任务分析】请提取询盘函相应典型句式。

＿＿＿＿＿＿＿＿＿＿＿＿＿＿＿＿＿＿＿＿＿＿＿＿＿＿＿＿＿＿＿＿＿＿

＿＿＿＿＿＿＿＿＿＿＿＿＿＿＿＿＿＿＿＿＿＿＿＿＿＿＿＿＿＿＿＿＿＿

＿＿＿＿＿＿＿＿＿＿＿＿＿＿＿＿＿＿＿＿＿＿＿＿＿＿＿＿＿＿＿＿＿＿

＿＿＿＿＿＿＿＿＿＿＿＿＿＿＿＿＿＿＿＿＿＿＿＿＿＿＿＿＿＿＿＿＿＿

＿＿＿＿＿＿＿＿＿＿＿＿＿＿＿＿＿＿＿＿＿＿＿＿＿＿＿＿＿＿＿＿＿＿

＿＿＿＿＿＿＿＿＿＿＿＿＿＿＿＿＿＿＿＿＿＿＿＿＿＿＿＿＿＿＿＿＿＿

＿＿＿＿＿＿＿＿＿＿＿＿＿＿＿＿＿＿＿＿＿＿＿＿＿＿＿＿＿＿＿＿＿＿

＿＿＿＿＿＿＿＿＿＿＿＿＿＿＿＿＿＿＿＿＿＿＿＿＿＿＿＿＿＿＿＿＿＿

学习任务二（2） 询盘 英文词汇学习

二、撰写询盘函

【制订方案】请阅读以下信息，并做相应翻译。

发货人：Victoria Glass Building Material CO.，LTD

收货人：Red Star Brick Joint Stock Company

产品：古典家具

交货条件：成本加运费

要求：20 英尺集装箱装运，通常情况下每月 35 个集装箱

重量：8 吨/集装箱

船公司：OOCL/APL

预计开船日：每周二、周三

装运港：深圳

卸货港：长滩

卸货地：Pawhusca，Elk City

所需服务：订舱、拖车、报检、报关

_____

_____

_____

_____

_____

【任务实施】请根据以上信息，自拟收发件人撰写询盘函。

_____

_____

_____

_____

_____

_____

_____

_____

学习活动 3　报盘函认知

学习目标

1. **知识目标**
    ◆能充分理解报盘函的概念。
    ◆能识记报盘函的内容。
    ◆能了解报盘函的特点。
2. **技能目标**
    ◆能识记报盘函的概念。
    ◆能复述报盘函的内容。
    ◆能识别报盘函。
3. **素养目标**
    ◆通过多样化学习方式提高自主学习能力，增强英语学习兴趣。
    ◆通过小组合作增强沟通表达能力，提高与国际客户沟通交流的信心。

学习课时

2 课时

学习过程

一、报盘函

【任务要求】报盘函包含哪些内容？（in English）

知识链接

1. offer（报盘函）

报盘函是指商务活动中作为卖方在接到客户的询价函后发出的回复性信函，是企业向顾客提供商品的有关交易条件的信函。报价函主要包括以下内容：①品名；②价格、数量；③结算方式；④发货期；⑤产品规模；⑥产品包装；⑦运输方式；等等。

2. specification（规格）

规格是指一般工业产品的物理形状，包括体积、长度、形状、重量等。商品规格是指一些足以反映商品品质的主要指标，如化学成分、含量、纯度、性能、容量、长短、粗细等。

3. discount（折扣）

折扣是指商品买卖中的让利、减价，是卖方给买方的价格优惠，但买卖双方给予或者接受折扣都要明示并如实入账。折扣的形式主要有两种：一是支付价款时对价款总额按一定比例即时予以扣除；二是在买方已支付价款总额后，卖方再按一定比例予以退还部分价款。这两种形式实质都是价格优惠，并无本质区别。

4. date of delivery（交货期）

交货期是指卖方将货物装上运往目的地（港）的运输工具或交付承运人的日期，习惯上称为"装运期"。

二、识读报盘函

【任务要求】请借助网络工具阅读以下信函，并翻译报盘函。

Sample Letter

Dear Mr. Parker,

We are pleased to receive your inquiry of November 20, 2010 and to learn that you are interested in our lady's leather bags No. 106, No. 136, No. 168 and No. 188. We would like to quote as follows：

Commodity	Article No.	CIF Houston Per PC
Lady's leather bags	106	USD 20.00
	136	USD 22.00
	168	USD 26.00
	188	USD 28.00

Packing: 1PC into a plastic bag, 10pcs into a carton.

Payment: by confirmed, irrevocable letter of credit payable by draft at sight.

Shipment: to be effected within 2 months from receipt of the relative L/C.

Insurance: to be covered by the seller for 110% of the invoice value covering all risks and war risk as per China insurance clauses.

We will keep this offer valid only for 10 days.

If you find the above acceptable, please fax us for confirmation as soon as possible.

Yours sincerely,

Liu Qiang

【任务分析】请小组讨论并回答以下问题。

1. What will be included in an offer? (reply in English)

_____

_____

2. What is the main idea of each paragraph? (reply in Chinese)

_____

_____

3. Translation: 非常遗憾我方不能供应所要求的货物。

请注意，我方报盘以你方下个月 30 日或之前确认为准。

_____

_____

_____

_____

4. Choose the best answer.

1) We offer you the following items _____ your reply reaching here by May 21 our time.

A. subjecting to　　　B. to subject to　　　C. subjects to　　　D. subject to

2）Our offer _____ firm till May 25.

A. could be　　　　　B. is　　　　　　　C. for　　　　　　　D. ／

3）FOB should be followed by _____ .

A. port of shipment　　　　　　　　　B. port of destination

C. port of transshipment　　　　　　　D. port of calls

4）In CIF, the _____ has to procure insurance against the buyer's risk of loss or damage to the goods during the carriage.

A. seller　　　　　　B. buyer　　　　　C. freight forwarder　　　D. receiver

【制订方案】请小组讨论，并根据商务信函三段式法则拟出以上报盘函语法知识点。

_____

_____

_____

_____

【任务实施】请采用专业角度翻译报盘函。

_____

_____

_____

_____

_____

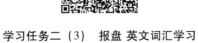

学习任务二（3）　报盘 英文词汇学习

学习活动 4　报盘函识读与撰写

学习目标

1. **知识目标**

◆能熟记国际货代报盘业务中涉及的专业术语。

◆能充分理解报盘函的写作内容。

◆能熟记报盘函的基本词汇。

2. **技能目标**

◆能熟练掌握商务信函三段式法则。

◆能熟练使用电脑，熟悉常用操作软件。

◆能识别函电中的特殊用语，根据中心词汇准确把握函电意图。

◆能够根据客户要求，运用英语灵活处理报盘函中的日常业务。

3. **素养目标**

◆通过情景模拟增强对工作岗位的认知感。

◆通过角色扮演及业务分析，提升工作岗位应变能力。

◆通过多样化学习方式提高自主学习能力，增强英语学习兴趣。

◆通过小组合作增强沟通表达能力，提高与国际客户沟通交流的信心。

学习课时

6 课时

学习过程

一、识读报盘函

（1）

From：Shraddha Sharma

To：heidi@ cc-cargo connection. com；Francis

Cc：RM；Amit；Signal Logistics

Sent：Saturday, February 07, 2009 6:02 PM

Subject：ocean freight charges：Shenzhen port to icd, tkd

Dear Heidi,

Good day to you.

Please advise us the best sea freight cost for the following enquiry.

Commodity：tiles

Requirement：20'ft containers：50 containers a month on regular basis. Importer is one of the biggest tiles companies in India.

Weight：27 tons each container

Port of loading：Shenzhen port

Port of discharge：Nhava Sheva port

Final destination：icd, tkd, New Delhi 1. A

We request you to please check and advise

1. Ocean freight and inland haulage in break up till icd, tkd, New Delhi；

2. Shipping line name, with transit time, sailing schedule；

3. Confirmation of 14 days free detention at final destination；

4. Validity of rates.

Heidi, please note this is one of the biggest account so we request you to please check with all direct shipping lines for the best costing. We have been following up this client for quite long and would really like to get his nomination.

Thanks in advance for the support.

With best regards,

Shraddha Sharma

Manager-Coordination & Operation

(2)

From: Heidi

To: Shraddha Sharma; Francis

Sent: Monday, February 09, 2009 10:17 AM

Subject: Re: ocean freight charges: Shenzhen port to icd, tkd

Dear Shraddha,

Can you advise the commodity and your ideal rate?

Regards,

HEIDIMA

CUSTOMER SERVICE MANAGER

CARGO CONNECTION WORLDWIDE LTD

RM1735, METRO CENTRE, PHASE I

21 LAM HING STREET KOWLOON BAY,

KOWLOON HONGKONG.

(3)

From: Shraddha Sharma

To: Heidi; Francis

Sent: Monday, February 09, 2009 2:20 PM

Subject: Re: ocean freight charges: Shenzhen port to icd, tkd

Dear Heidi,

Good day to you.

Commodity is tiles. We have no idea of the rates but they are very low.

With best regards,

Shraddha Sharma

Manager—Coordination & Operation

(4)

From: Heidi

Sent: 2009-02-09 16:29:54

To: Shraddha Sharma; Francis; Jennifer Ye

Cc: RM; Amit; Signal Logistics

Subject: Re: ocean freight charges: Shenzhen port to icd, tkd

Dear Jennifer,

Please check our best cost to the agent as soon as possible.

Regards,

HEIDIMA

CUSTOMER SERVICE MANAGER

（5）

From：Jennifer Ye

To：Shraddha Sharma；Francis；Heidi

Sent：Tuesday February 10，2009 11：09 AM

Subject：Re；ocean freight charges：Shenzhen port to icd，tkd

Dear Shraddha，

This is Jennifer. We are glad to list our net/net rate ex Shenzhen to icd，tkd，New Delhi as below.

Carrier：HAPAG-LLOYD

Ocean freight：USD420+660/2O（O/F+INLAND）

CY closing：Tue

ETD：Thu

T/T：appx. 20 days

Via：Nhava Sheva

Max goods weight：27 tons

Validity：28. 02. 2009

Remark：14 days free detention at final destination but carrier cannot accept freight collect for the 2nd route from Nhava Sheva to tkd，New Delhi

Carrier：OOCL

Ocean freight：USD350+950/20（O/F+INLAND）

CY closing：Mon

ETD：Wed

T/T：appx. 20 days

Via：Nhava Sheva

Max goods weight：27 tons

Validity：28. 02. 2009

Remark：14 days free detention at final destination and carrier accept freight collect for the 2nd route from Nhava Sheva to tkd，New Delhi.

The rate is based on 50 containers a month on regular basis. Subject to local charges at both ends.

Have any further information，please advise. Thanks.

JENNIFER YE

CUSTOMER SERVICES

【任务分析】请认真阅读信函，并根据信函回答以下问题。

1. Where is the letter from and to? (Letter 1)

_____

2. Where will the goods be loaded and discharged respectively? (Letter 1)

_____

3. Where will the goods finally go to? (Letter 1)

_____

4. How long will the detention period be at the final destination? (Letter 1)

_____

5. What does Shraddha request at the end of the letter? (Letter 1)

_____

6. Who is in charge of booking space? (Letter 5)

_____

7. What does Heidi want Jennifer to do? (Letter 5)

_____

8. How many carriers are recommended by the forwarding company? What are they? (Letter 5)

_____

9. Which carrier accepts freight collect for the 2nd route from Nhava Sheva to tkd, New Delhi? (Letter 5)

_____

【任务分析】请根据信函完成下列信息空白处的填写。

Shraddha Sharma requests Heidi to advise the best 1. _____ cost. She asks for detailed information in the letter, including 2. _____ , 3. _____ , 4. _____ , and 5. _____ . In addition, Sharaddha notes that this shipment is one of the largest 6. _____ and wish to get the 7. _____ .

In Letters 2 & 3, Heidi asks Shraddha to advise the 8. _____ and the ideal rate. Shraddha confirms that the commodity is 9. _____ but he has no exact idea about 10. _____ .

In Letters 4 & 5, 11. _____ asks 12. _____ to check the best cost to the agent as soon as possible. Jennifer lists the net/net rate ex 13. _____ to 14. _____ .

She recommended 15. _____ carriers. However Carrier HAPAG－LLOYD only agrees 16. _____ days free detention but doesn't accept freight collect for the 2nd route from Nhava Sheva to tkd.

学习任务二（4）　报盘 英文词汇学习

二、撰写报盘函

【制订方案】请阅读以下信息，并做相应翻译。

背景资料：

深圳××物流有限公司业务员 Sally 提供了船运公司报价

承运人：ANL（Austalin National Line）

运费：USD 1 450+800/20'（海洋运费+内陆运费）

截关日：星期一到星期三

预计开船日期：星期四

航程：大约 20 天

转经：长滩

最大载重量：18 吨

有效期：2009 年 11 月 28 日

备注：货到目的地后可免费堆仓 14 天，关于第二程从长滩到内陆的运费，承运人不接受运费到付。

另：此次报价基于每月 50 箱的柜量，以起运港和目的港的收费为准。

◆请翻译背景资料：

_____

_____

_____

_____

◆请翻译以下句子：

我们很高兴收到你们 10 月 6 日的询盘，并且很高兴地了解到你们对我们的服务感兴趣。(be pleased to ... and to learn that ...)

按您的要求，我们很高兴为您做以下的报价。(At your request, ... take pleasure in ... as follows / the following ...)

在 11 月前我们将会保持报盘有效。(keep valid for/before ...)

【任务实施】请根据以上信息，以深圳××物流有限公司业务员 Sally 的身份写报盘信给 Mary，涵盖背景资料的内容。

学习任务三　确认信息函

工作情境描述

　　Joey 在深圳某货运代理公司完成为期两周的企业培训后，经理要求其在部门岗位间轮岗一个月，现就职于客服人员岗位。其工作内容是与客户通过信函确认地址及贸易条款、运费与运输方式、单据内容、运输路线和时间等。

学习任务解析

　　学习任务见图 3-1。

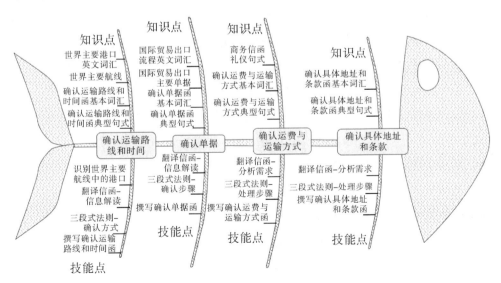

图 3-1　学习任务

24 课时

学习活动 1　确认运输路线和时间

学习活动 2　确认单据

学习活动 3　确认运费与运输方式

学习活动 4　确认具体地址和条款

学习活动 1　确认运输路线和时间

1. **知识目标**

◆能熟记国际货代业务中涉及的专业术语。

◆能熟记世界主要港口的英文词汇（亚洲、美洲）。

◆能识别世界主要航线（亚洲、美洲）。

◆能识记确认运输路线和时间函基本词汇。

◆能掌握确认运输路线和时间函典型句式。

2. **技能目标**

◆能熟练掌握商务信函三段式法则。

◆能熟练使用电脑，熟悉常用操作软件。

◆能识别函电中的特殊用语，根据中心词汇准确把握函电意图。

◆能够根据客户要求，运用英语灵活处理确认运输路线和时间函中的日常业务。

3. **素养目标**

◆通过情景模拟增强对工作岗位的认知感。

◆通过角色扮演及业务分析，提升工作岗位应变能力。

◆通过多样化学习方式提高自主学习能力，增强英语学习兴趣。

◆通过小组合作增强沟通表达能力，提高与国际客户沟通交流的信心。

学习课时

2 课时

学习过程

一、熟记世界主要港口

【任务要求】请识记以下港口的英文名称以及其所属国家或地区。

2020 年世界十大港口（中国占七席）：

第一名 上海港：_____

第二名 新加坡港：_____

第三名 深圳港：_____

第四名 宁波港：_____

第五名 维多利亚港：_____

第六名 釜山港：_____

第七名 广州港：_____

第八名 青岛港：_____

第九名 迪拜港：_____

第十名 天津港：_____

世界其他主要港口：

（1）鹿特丹港：_____

（2）纽约港：_____

（3）神户港：_____

（4）新奥尔良港：_____

（5）横滨港：_____

（6）马赛港：＿＿＿＿＿＿＿＿＿＿＿＿＿＿＿＿＿

（7）新加坡港：＿＿＿＿＿＿＿＿＿＿＿＿＿＿＿

（8）安特卫普港：＿＿＿＿＿＿＿＿＿＿＿＿＿＿

（9）伦敦港：＿＿＿＿＿＿＿＿＿＿＿＿＿＿＿＿

（10）汉堡港：＿＿＿＿＿＿＿＿＿＿＿＿＿＿＿＿

知识链接

1. Singapore（新加坡）

新加坡港位于新加坡共和国（The Republic of Singapore）的南部沿海，西临马六甲海峡（Straits of Malacca）的东南侧，南临新加坡海峡的北侧，是亚太地区的第二大港口，世界沿海港口行业中比较知名，也是世界最大的集装箱港口之一。该港扼太平洋及印度洋之间的航运要道，战略地位十分重要。它自 13 世纪开始便是国际贸易港口，已发展成为国际著名的转口港。新加坡港也是该国的政治、经济、文化及交通的中心。

2. Busan/Pusan（釜山）

釜山港位于韩国（Republic of Korea）东南沿海，东南濒朝鲜（Korea）海峡，西临洛东（Naktong）江，与日本对马岛相峙，是韩国最大的港口，也是世界第六大集装箱港。始建于 1876 年，在 20 世纪初由于京釜铁路的通车而迅速发展起来。它是韩国海陆空交通的枢纽，也是金融和商业中心，在韩国的对外贸易中发挥着重要作用。工业仅次于首尔，其他产业还有纺织、汽车轮胎、石油加工、机械、化工、食品、木材加工、水产品加工、造船和汽车等，其中机械工业尤为发达，造船、轮胎生产居韩国首位，出口水产品在出口贸易中占有重要位置。港口距机场约 28 千米。

3. Dubai（迪拜）

迪拜港又名拉希德港（Mina Rashid），位于阿联酋（The United Arab Emirates）东北沿海，濒临波斯湾南侧，与 1981 年新建的米纳杰贝勒阿里港（Mina Jebel Ali）同属迪拜港务局管辖。迪拜港是阿联酋最大的港口，也是集装箱大港之一。迪拜港口在世界港口中比较闻名，该港地处亚欧非三大洲的交汇点，是中东地区最大的自由贸易港，以转口贸易发达而著称。它是海湾地区的修船中心，拥有名列前茅的百万吨级的干船坞。主要工业有造船、塑料、炼铝、海水淡化、轧钢及车辆装配等，还有年产 50 万吨的水泥厂。长期以来，该港都是波斯湾南岸的商业中心。它有该国最大的迪拜国际机场，每天有定期航班飞往世界各地。

迪拜港主要码头泊位有 18 个，岸线长 4 265 米，最大水深 13.5 米，装卸设备包括各种岸吊、可移式吊、集装箱门吊、装卸桥、跨运车及滚装设施等，其中集装箱门吊最大起重能力达 40 吨。油码头最大可停靠载重 7 万吨的油船，有油管与油罐相接。港区有钢架转运货棚长达 1 460 米，还拥有带有空调的集装箱仓库，外加能承接与分流各种商品的货场，包括石油制品、易腐烂品、汽车、冷藏品及木材等。迪拜政府为了鼓励转口业务，规定在自由贸易区免税存入仓库，入关后再出口（转口）的商品给予全部退税。其主要出口货物除石油外，还有天然气、铝锭、石油化工产品及土特产等，进口货物主要有粮食、机械及消费品。

二、熟记世界主要航线

【任务要求】熟记世界主要航线及港口。

五大洋：_____

七大洲：_____

世界三大主要集装箱航线：

远东—北美航线（太平洋航线）

_____

_____

北美—欧洲（地中海航线）

_____

_____

远东—欧洲（地中海航线）

_____

_____

_____

三、识读确认运输路线和时间函

From：John Binh – Cargo Connection
To：Jennifer Ye；magielinecc-cargonnection.
Subject：Re：FCL inquiry：Jiangmen to Oklahoma，USA
2021-03-13 09:36:54

Dear Jennifer，

Today we checked with Hanjin Shipping USA and they told us they do not have a railroad hub in Oklahoma City，most of their Oklahoma cargo is being shipped to Dallas，TX railroad hub first，and then delivered to Oklahoma City by truck. So most likely Hanjin can offer you a door delivery rate，which includes the destination delivery rates.

Please double check with Hanjin if Ocean freight：USD 3 490/20'GP is from China to Oklahoma rail/truck hub？ or to door OK 74055？ or to Dallas only？ We are confused.
Waiting for your quick confirmation.

Best regards，
John

【任务要求】请借助网络工具阅读信函，并翻译信函。
【任务分析】
◆Answer the following questions according to the letter.

1. What is John confused about?

_____

_____

2. What is the possible route for Hanjin Shipping USA to carry the cargo to Oklahoma City?

_____

_____

3. To which city can the goods of Hanjin be directly shipped according to the letter?

_____

_____

4. What does John want Jennifer to do?

_____

_____

◆Complete the blanks according to the information given below.

John Binh informs Jennifer that Hanjin Shipping USA has no 1. _____ in Oklahoma City after checking, but the majority of their 2. _____ is being shipped to 3. _____, TX railroad hub first, and then delivered by truck to 4. _____. So John Binh asks Jennifer to 5. _____ with Hanjin what the rate means: by 6. _____, 7. _____ or to 8. _____.

【制订方案】请小组讨论，拟出以上信函的语法知识点和段落大意。

_____

_____

_____

_____

【任务实施】请运用专业角度翻译信函。

_____

_____

_____

_____

_____

_____

_____

_____

学习任务三（1）　信息确认函 英文词汇学习

四、撰写确认运输路线和时间函

【任务要求】撰写确认信息函。

背景资料：

香港××物流有限公司业务员 Mary 发现 COSCO 的报价比其他两家船运公司高出两倍，联系后得知它们在 Owasso 没有集散中心，货物运到 Los Angeles 港口后，需用铁路运到 Owasso 火车站。

实训任务：

请以香港××物流有限公司业务员 Mary 的身份告诉××物流公司业务员 Sally 上述信息，让她跟 COSCO 确认此次报价是从广州到 Owasso 火车站，还是到邮编 0W 89006 所属城市的到门服务。

【任务分析】请分析并回答以下问题。

1. 背景资料中的卸货港和最终目的地是哪里，属于哪个国家？

_____

2. 背景资料中的起运港是哪里，属于哪个国家？

_____

3. What is the carrier's name?

_____

4. 翻译：铁路货物集散中心。

_____

5. Who will be the sender and receiver in your reply letter?

_____

【制订方案】请小组讨论，并根据商务信函三段式法则拟出确认信息函的段落大意（即信函提纲）。

_____

_____

【任务实施】请根据以上信息，撰写确认运输路线函。

_____

_____

_____
_____
_____
_____
_____
_____
_____
_____
_____
_____
_____
_____
_____
_____
_____
_____
_____
_____

学习活动 2　确认单据

学习目标

1. **知识目标**

◆能熟记国际贸易出口流程。

◆能熟记国际贸易主要单据类型。

◆能熟记确认单据函的基本词汇。

◆能掌握确认单据函的典型句式。

2. 技能目标

　　◆能识别函电中的特殊用语，根据中心词汇准确把握函电意图。

　　◆能够根据客户要求，运用英语灵活处理确认单据函中的日常业务。

3. 素养目标

　　◆通过各种学习工具提高自主学习能力，增强英语学习兴趣。

　　◆通过情景模拟增强对工作岗位的认知感，提高与国际客户沟通交流的信心。

　　◆通过小组合作增强沟通表达能力，培养团结合作精神，提高工作抗压能力。

学习课时

8 课时

学习过程

一、熟记国际贸易出口流程和主要单据类型

【任务要求】请翻译以下专业术语。

insurance

shipping space booking

customs declaration form

prepare goods and inspection

letter of credit

sign the contract

cancel after verification drawback

invoice

form E/A、C/O

application of inspection and quarantine certificate

shipping order

packing list

picking outbound

contract

customs collection

bill of exchange

making documents and foreign exchange settlement

transportation

【任务要求】请为以上的国际贸易主要单据按照出口贸易流程分门别类。

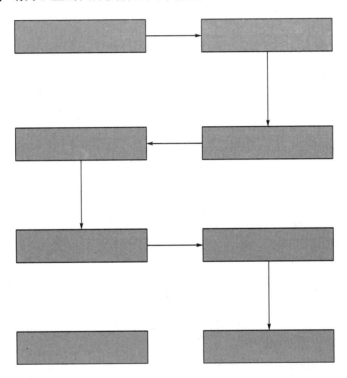

【任务要求】请翻译并按以下类别将文件进行归类：

① official document：_____

② commercial document：_____

③ freight document：_____

a. import licence

b. commercial invoice

c. mate's receipt

d. bill of exchange of draft

e. forwarders certificate of receipt（FCR，货运代理人收讫货物证明）

f. verified gross mass（VGM，核实集装箱总重）

g. customs declaration form（报关单）

h. debit note（借记单、借记通知）

i. shipping order（订舱单）

j. packing list

k. export tax rebate form（出口退税表）

l. bill of lading

m. letter of credit

n. insurance policy

o. container load plan（集装箱装载计划表）

p. booking note（订舱委托书）

q. certificate of Iso Soc Tank（国际标准 Soc 储罐证书）

r. export licence

s. inspection of certificate

t. contract

u. air waybill（空运单）

v. shipper's letter of instruction（托运人托运说明书）

w. delivery order（交货单）

x. equipment interchange receipt（设备交接单）

y. form A（普惠制原产地证明书格式 A）

z. certificate of origin（原产地证书）

学习任务三（2） 进出口文件名称 英文词汇学习

二、识读确认单据函

From：John Binh-Cargo connection

Sent：2021-03-17 14:25:45

To：Jennifer Ye；antonychen@ cc-cargo connection. com

Subject：FCL inquiry：Jiangmen to Oklahoma, USA

Dear Jennifer,

For this shipment, can I issue HBL in Vietnam? You will provide me details for HBL issuance from shipper's information.

I will provide all details for MBL and AMS filing.

Can you check with Hanjin if they can file rule "10+2" on behalf of importer? If not, we will have customs broker in the USA to deal with the paperwork.

Thanks a lot and regards,

John

From：Jennifer Ye

To：John Binh-Cargo connection；

Sent：Tuesday, March 17, 2009 3:01 AM

Subject：FCL inquiry：Jiangmen to Oklahoma, USA

Dear John,

It is switch bill, right? Please confirm.

AMS must be finished in Shenzhen and you can ask your customs broker to do "10+2" in USA. Kindly note. Thanks.

Jennifer Ye

【任务要求】请借助网络工具阅读信函，并翻译信函。

【任务分析】

◆Answer the following questions according to the letter.

1. Who will issue HBL?

_____

_____

_____

_____

2. Who will issue MBL?

_____

_____

_____

_____

3. Who will file for AMS? And where?

_____

_____

_____

_____

4. Who will file for rule "10+2"? And where?

_____

_____

_____

_____

◆Complete the blanks according to the information given below.

John wants to issue _____ for the shipment in Vietnam and requires Jennifer to provide details for it, and he will offer Jennifer all details for _____ and _____. And also, John asks Jennifer to check whether Hanjin can file _____ in the name of the importer. If Hanjin cannot, John will turn to _____ to see to the paperwork. In reply, Jennifer asks John to confirm that it is _____, and advises that

AMS should be finished in ＿＿＿＿＿＿＿ and "10+2" should be done by ＿＿＿＿＿＿

in USA.

【制订方案】请小组讨论，拟出以上信函的语法知识点和信函大意。

＿＿＿＿＿＿＿＿＿＿＿＿＿＿＿＿＿＿＿＿＿＿＿＿＿＿＿＿＿＿＿＿＿＿＿＿＿＿

＿＿＿＿＿＿＿＿＿＿＿＿＿＿＿＿＿＿＿＿＿＿＿＿＿＿＿＿＿＿＿＿＿＿＿＿＿＿

＿＿＿＿＿＿＿＿＿＿＿＿＿＿＿＿＿＿＿＿＿＿＿＿＿＿＿＿＿＿＿＿＿＿＿＿＿＿

＿＿＿＿＿＿＿＿＿＿＿＿＿＿＿＿＿＿＿＿＿＿＿＿＿＿＿＿＿＿＿＿＿＿＿＿＿＿

【任务实施】请翻译信函。

＿＿＿＿＿＿＿＿＿＿＿＿＿＿＿＿＿＿＿＿＿＿＿＿＿＿＿＿＿＿＿＿＿＿＿＿＿＿

＿＿＿＿＿＿＿＿＿＿＿＿＿＿＿＿＿＿＿＿＿＿＿＿＿＿＿＿＿＿＿＿＿＿＿＿＿＿

＿＿＿＿＿＿＿＿＿＿＿＿＿＿＿＿＿＿＿＿＿＿＿＿＿＿＿＿＿＿＿＿＿＿＿＿＿＿

＿＿＿＿＿＿＿＿＿＿＿＿＿＿＿＿＿＿＿＿＿＿＿＿＿＿＿＿＿＿＿＿＿＿＿＿＿＿

＿＿＿＿＿＿＿＿＿＿＿＿＿＿＿＿＿＿＿＿＿＿＿＿＿＿＿＿＿＿＿＿＿＿＿＿＿＿

＿＿＿＿＿＿＿＿＿＿＿＿＿＿＿＿＿＿＿＿＿＿＿＿＿＿＿＿＿＿＿＿＿＿＿＿＿＿

＿＿＿＿＿＿＿＿＿＿＿＿＿＿＿＿＿＿＿＿＿＿＿＿＿＿＿＿＿＿＿＿＿＿＿＿＿＿

＿＿＿＿＿＿＿＿＿＿＿＿＿＿＿＿＿＿＿＿＿＿＿＿＿＿＿＿＿＿＿＿＿＿＿＿＿＿

＿＿＿＿＿＿＿＿＿＿＿＿＿＿＿＿＿＿＿＿＿＿＿＿＿＿＿＿＿＿＿＿＿＿＿＿＿＿

＿＿＿＿＿＿＿＿＿＿＿＿＿＿＿＿＿＿＿＿＿＿＿＿＿＿＿＿＿＿＿＿＿＿＿＿＿＿

＿＿＿＿＿＿＿＿＿＿＿＿＿＿＿＿＿＿＿＿＿＿＿＿＿＿＿＿＿＿＿＿＿＿＿＿＿＿

From：Maggielin［mailto：maggielin@ cc-cargo connection. com］
Sent：Wednesday，1 April 2009 8:30 AM
To：Eric Gunawan（CIL Surabaya）；Jennifer Ye；Antonychen；Heidi
Subject：RE：new air-shipment of PT Panggung to Surabaya

Dear Eric，

Good morning！

The shipper just informed us that the original packing list & invoice is not needed for this shipment. Please kindly check with consignee and advise.

Waiting for your soonest reply, thanks a lot！

Best regards，

Maggie lin

From：Eric Gunawan
Sent：Wednesday，April 01，2009 9:48 AM maggielin@ cc-cargo connection. com；
To：Jennifer Ye；antonychen；Heidi
Subject：RE：new air-shipment of PT Panggung to Surabaya

Dear Maggie，

Please tell the shipper that without the original docs attached to the goods there will be clearance delay in Indonesia as Indonesian customs requires original invoice and packing list. If the consignee has to wait the docs couriered to them，then the cargoes will have arrived and still waiting for the original docs from China. This will incur extra airport storage charges. Anyway，I will pass on this info to the consignee. I just want to make things simple rather than disturbing consignee all the times as this is part of our service.

Best regards，

Eric

【任务要求】请借助网络工具阅读信函，并翻译信函。

【任务分析】

◆Answer the following questions according to the letter.

1. What did Maggie ask Eric to do in the first letter?

2. What will happen if the cargo arrives at Indonesia without original documents?

_____

_____

3. What loss will they suffer if the cargoes have arrived without the original docs from China?

_____

_____

4. Who will pay for the airport storage charge if it happens in this shipment?

_____

_____

◆Complete the blanks according to the information given below.

Maggie notes from shipper that the original _____ and _____ are not needed for the shipment. _____ tells Maggie that without original documents attached to the goods _____ will happen, because Indonesian _____ requires original documents. If the goods arrive without original documents, extra _____ will occur.

【制订方案】请小组讨论，拟出以上信函的语法知识点和专业术语。

_____

_____

_____

_____

【任务实施】请翻译信函。

_____

_____

_____

_____

_____

_____

_____

_____

_____

_____

_____

_____

_____

_____

_____

_____

_____

_____

_____

三、撰写确认单据函

【任务要求】撰写确认清关单据函。

背景资料：

托运人 John 致函深圳××国际物流公司货代员 Sally，告知对方清关文件已经寄出，但提单上显示的起飞日期和之前邮件所说的不一致，John 询问是否以提单日期为准。另外，John 请 Sally 提供此批货的实际重量、体积和收费重量。

实训任务：

请以托运人 John 的身份写信给货代员 Sally，内容涵盖背景资料中的内容。

【任务分析】请分析并回答以下问题。

1. 翻译：清关文件。

_____

2. 翻译：起飞日期。

_____

3. 翻译：之前的；以……为准。

_____

4. 翻译：实际重量、体积；收费重量。

5. 根据商务信函三段式法则拟出回复函的段落大意。

【制订方案】请小组讨论并根据商务信函三段式法则拟出中文回复函。

【任务实施】请根据以上信息，撰写确认单据函。

学习任务三（3）　确认单据 英文词汇学习

学习活动3 确认运费与运输方式

学习目标

1. **知识目标**

◆能熟记英文商务信函礼仪句式。

◆能熟记确认运费与运输方式函的基本词汇。

◆能掌握确认运费与运输方式函的典型句式。

2. **技能目标**

◆能熟练掌握商务信函三段式法则。

◆能识别函电中的特殊用语，根据中心词汇准确把握函电意图。

◆能够根据客户要求，运用英语灵活处理确认运费与运输方式函中的日常业务。

3. **素养目标**

◆通过各种学习工具提高自主学习能力，增强英语学习兴趣。

◆通过情景模拟增强对工作岗位的认知感，提高与国际客户沟通交流的信心。

◆通过小组合作增强沟通表达能力，培养团结合作精神，提高工作抗压能力。

4. **思政目标**

◆通过不断的训练和中国礼仪的熏陶，提升商务礼仪认知。

学习课时

4课时

学习过程

一、熟记商务信函礼仪典型句式

【任务要求】请翻译以下典型句式。

We are very much pleased to inform you that …

In reply to your letter of 31 Oct., we …

We are writing to ask about the shipment to be loaded next week.

With great delight we learn that …

Thank you very much for your prompt reply.

We wish to extend our appreciation for your kind offer/attention.

Many thanks for your last kind letter.

Your letter which arrived this morning gave us great delight, as you know …

First of all, we must thank you for your kindness to us and for your compliments.

We were glad to receive your letter of …

We hope to receive your favor at an early date.

We await the favor of your early/prompt reply.

We trust that you will reply us immediately.

Please feel free to contact us for further information.

Your kind early reply will be highly appreciated.

Waiting for your soonest reply.

We are looking forward to receiving your early reply.

We look forward to our next order soon.

Thanks for your sincere cooperation with us.

Thank you again for your kind consideration of our request.

二、识读确认运费与运输方式函

From：John Binh-Cargo Connection
Sent：March 13, 2009 14:41:37
To：Jennifer Ye；magielin@ cc cargoconnection. com
Subject：Re：FCL inquiry：Jiangmen to Oklahoma, USA
Dear Jennifer,
How much is total cost to OK 74055?
Thanks and regards,
John

From：Jennifer Ye
Sent：March 13, 2009 16:44:26
To：John Binh Cargo Connection；maggielin@ cccargoconnection. commaggielin@ cc-cargo connection. com
Subject：Re：FCL inquirv：Jiangmen to Oklahoma, USA

Dear John,
We need recheck rate to OK 74055. Kindlyawait. Thanks.
Best regards,
Jennifer Ye

From：Jennifer Ye
To：John Binh-Cargo Connection；maggielin@ cc-cargo connection. com
Sent：Friday, March 13, 2009 1:41 AM
Subject Re：FCL inquiry：Jiangmen to Oklahoma, USA

Dear John,
As per your request, we are glad to provide net/net rate ex Jiangmen to OK 74055 as below：
Carrier：MSC
Ocean freight：USD 3 790/20 GP
CY closing：From Mon to Wed (barge)
ETD：Tue (Chiwan)
T/T：appx. 26 days
Validity：end of Mar
Subject to local charge at both ends.
Best regards,
Jennifer Ye

【任务要求】请借助网络工具阅读信函，并翻译信函。

【任务分析】

◆Answer the following questions according to the letter.

1. Where is OK 74055, in Oklahoma City or Owasso City?

_____

2. How many carriers has Jennifer recommended till now?

_____

3. Why does Jennifer change Carrier Hanjin into Carrier MSC?

_____

4. When and to which port will MSC depart from Shenzhen?

_____

◆Complete the blanks according to the information given below.

John inquires about the _____ to _____. Jennifer informs him that they need to check the _____ again. Jennifer then offers net rate ex _____ to _____, including the following information: _____, _____, _____, _____, _____, and validity.

【制订方案】请小组讨论，拟出以上信函的语法知识点和翻译第 3 篇信函。

_____

_____

_____

_____

_____

_____

_____

【任务实施】请翻译信函大意。

学习任务三（4）　确认运费 英文词汇学习

学习活动 4　确认具体地址和条款

学习目标

1. 知识目标

◆能熟记确认具体地址和条款函的基本词汇。

◆能掌握确认具体地址和条款函的典型句式。

2. 技能目标

　　◆能熟练掌握商务信函三段式法则。

　　◆能识别函电中的特殊用语，根据中心词汇准确把握函电意图。

　　◆能够根据客户要求，运用英语灵活处理确认具体地址和条款函中的日常业务。

3. 素养目标

　　◆通过各种学习工具提高自主学习能力，增强英语学习兴趣。

　　◆通过情景模拟增强对工作岗位的认知感，提高与国际客户沟通交流的信心。

　　◆通过小组合作增强沟通表达能力，培养团结合作精神，提高工作抗压能力。

学习课时

4 课时

学习过程

一、识读确认地址函

（1）
From：Jennifer Ye
To：John Binh-Cargo Connection；
Sent：Monday, March 23, 2009 12:52 AM
Subject：Re：FCL inquiry：Jiangmen to Oklahoma, USA

Dear John,
The carrier informed that we must offer zip code of Oklahoma city for booking this shipmen due to it is to door service.
Please advise ZIP code which belongs to Oklahoma city instead of Owasso city. Kindly not-
Thanks.
Best regards,
Jennifer Ye

（2）

From：John Binh-Cargo Connection

Sent：2009-03-23 16：54：49

To：Jennifer Ye；antonychen@ cc-cargo connection. com

Subject：Re：FCL inquiry：Jiangmen to Oklahoma, USA

Dear Jennifer,

We advised zip code in previous e-mail already. Anyway, we provide it again OK 74055.

Thanks a lot and best regards,

John

（3）

From：Jennifer Ye

To：John Binh Cargo Connection；antonychen@ cc-cargo connection. com

Sent：Monday, March 23, 2009 1：16 AM

Subject：Re：FCL inquiry：Jiangmen to Oklahoma, USA

Dear John,

We advised you on our 12th March e-mail that OK 74055 is not in Oklahoma city, it belongs Owasso city. Kindly note.

Best regards,

Jennifer Ye

（4）

From：John Binh Cargo Connection

Sent：2009-03-23 17：20：56

To：Jennifer Ye；antonychen@ cc-cargo connection. com

Subject：Re：FCL inquiry：Jiangmen to Oklahoma, USA

Dear Jennifer,

Noted your message. Thank you for your e-mail.

Best regards,

John

（5）

From：Jennifer Ye

To：John Binh Cargo Connection；antonychen@ cc-cargo connection. com

Sent：Monday, March 23, 2009 1:28 AM

Subject：Re：FCL inquiry：Jiangmen to Oklahoma, USA

Dear John,

We must provide the correct ZIP code to Hanjin in order to run this shipment. Please advise this information as early as you can. Thanks.

Best regards,

Jennifer Ye

（6）

From：John Binh Cargo Connection

Sent：2009-03-23 17：43：15

To：Jennifer Ye；antonychen@ cc-cargo connection. com

Subject：Re：FCL inquiry：Jiangmen to Oklahoma, USA

Dear Jennifer,

Please book with Hanjin to Oklahoma terminal as per previous confirmation.

I do not know why Hanjin request us another zip code while there is only one zip code. Here is full consignee address：

Tile Shack Mosaic Supplies.

7762-A N. Owasso Expy

Owasso, OK 74055

Please assist！

Thanks and regards,

John

(7)

From: Jennifer Ye

To: John Binh Cargo Connection; antonychen@ cc-cargo connection. com

Sent: Monday, March 23, 2009 6:04 AM

Subject: Re: FCL inquiry: Jiangmen to Oklahoma, USA

Dear John,

As per our prior e-mail, it is to door (Oklahoma City) rate from Hanjin. So we must offer zip code to Hanji.

If your final destination is OK 74055, the nearest POD should be Tulsa instead of Oklahoma City. You can check the map at the address below:

http://maps.yahoo.com Lahoma %20 city %2 COK

Waiting for your information. Thanks.

Best regards,

Jennifer Ye

---

(8)

From: John Binh-Cargo Connection

Sent: 2009-03-24 07: 52: 05

To: Jennifer Ye; antonychen@ cc-cargoconnection. com

Subject: Re: FCL inquiry: Jiangmen to Oklahoma, USA

Dear Jennifer,

Please arrange the freight to Tulsa. Let us know if Hanjin can provide this service. Thank you.

Look forward to hearing from you.

Best regards,

John

（9）

From：Jennifer Ye

Sent：2009-03-24 09：38：21

To：John Binh Cargo Connection；

Subject：Re：FCL inquiry：Jiangmen to Oklahoma，USA

Dear John，Noted but Hanjin could not provide to Tulsa ramp service，it is to door（Tulsa）service only. Please note.

We are checking other carrier from Jiangmen to Tulsa. Kindlyawait.

Best regards，

Jennifer Ye

【任务要求】请借助网络工具阅读信函，并翻译信函。

【任务分析】

◆Answer the following questions according to the letter.

1. What's wrong with the zip code? Why does the carrier want the zip code once again?

_____

_____

2. What is the final destination of the freight?

_____

_____

3. Which is the nearest POD for the freight to Owasso?

_____

_____

4. What is John's final decision about the freight?

_____

_____

◆Complete the blanks according to the information given below.

In the letter，Jennifer asked John to provide the correct 1. _____ of the city because the freight is 2. _____ service. John confirmed that the final destination is 3. _____ .Jennifer informs that if the freight goes to the given zip code address，the

nearest POD would be 4. _____ instead of 5. _____.

【制订方案】请小组讨论，拟出以上信函的语法知识点和翻译第 6 篇和第 7 篇信函。

_____
_____
_____
_____
_____
_____
_____
_____
_____
_____

【任务实施】请翻译信函大意。

_____
_____
_____
_____
_____

二、撰写确认运费及支付方式函

【任务要求】撰写确认运费及支付方式函。

背景资料：

香港××物流有限公司 Mary 告知深圳××物流公司货代员 Sally，发货人会提供整套出口报关单据，收货人会在当天下订单给发货方，并在一周内以信用证方式支付货款，请落实具体报检费用。另外，收货人想确定整个运输过程所需的费用，不希望有任何额外费用的增加。

货代员 Sally 回复 Mary，告知对方报检会产生额外费用，但目前还无法得知具体费用信息，请耐心等待相关消息。

实训任务：

1. 请以货代员 Mary 的身份致函 Sally，告知背景资料中的相关信息。

2. 请以货代员 Sally 的身份回复 Mary。

【任务分析】请分析并回答以下问题。

1. 翻译：整套出口报关单据。

2. 翻译：与某人下订单（造句）。

3. 翻译：以信用证方式付款。

4. 翻译：具体报检费用。

5. 翻译：整个运输过程。

6. 根据商务信函三段式法则拟出回复函段落大意。

【制订方案】请小组讨论并根据商务信函三段式法则拟出中文回复函。

【任务实施】请根据以上信息，撰写确认运费及支付方式函。

_____

_____

_____

_____

_____

_____

_____

_____

_____

_____

_____

_____

_____

_____

_____

_____

_____

_____

_____

_____

_____

学习任务三（5）确认运费 英文词汇学习

学习任务四　还盘函

Joey 在深圳某货运代理公司业务员岗位，经过为期一周的市场开发业务，收到了多封来自客户的信函，现需要一一进行还盘，如价格、重量或其他费用等。

学习任务解析

学习任务见图 4-1。

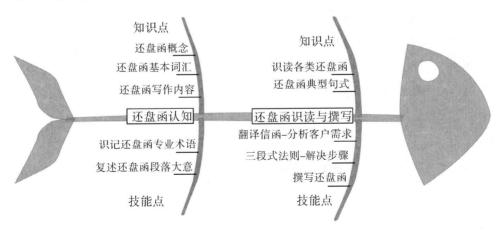

图 4-1　学习任务

建议课时

16 课时

工作流程与活动

学习活动 1　还盘函认知

学习活动 2　还盘函识读与撰写

学习活动 1　还盘函认知

学习目标

1. **知识目标**

　◆能充分理解还盘函的概念。

　◆能识记还盘函的基本词汇。

　◆能识记还盘函的写作内容。

2. **技能目标**

　◆能识记询盘函的专业术语。

　◆能复述还盘函的段落大意。

3. **素养目标**

　◆通过多样化学习方式提高自主学习能力，增强英语学习兴趣。

学习课时

2 课时

学习过程

一、熟记国际贸易中还盘函的专业术语

【任务要求】请识记以下国际贸易中还盘函的专业术语。

还盘_____

参考价_____

现行价_____

开盘价_____

收盘价_____

合理价格_____

特殊价格_____

差价_____

品质以卖方样品为准_____

品质以买方样品为准_____

净重_____

毛重_____

皮重_____

竞争性价格_____

批发价_____

零售价_____

制造人、工厂主、制造商_____

降价_____

让步、让与物_____

下降、婉拒、谢绝_____

现实的、实际的_____

偏高_____

例外的、异常的_____

达成交易_____

由于_____

二、理解还盘函的写作内容

【任务要求】请复述还盘函的段落大意。

_____

_____

_____

_____

_____

知识链接

counter-offer（还盘）

还盘是受盘人对发盘内容不完全同意而提出修改或变更的表示。在国际贸易中，出口方发盘后自然希望对方直接同意而不进行还盘，但这几乎是不可能的。在激烈的竞争环境中，反复讨价还价，发盘、还盘、再还盘……是常有事，有时甚至会经历几十个回合才能达成最后交易。

出口方报价，进口方还盘后，出口方应做出答复。答复可以是完全接受对方的还盘，此时交易即告达成；也可以是完全拒绝对方的还盘而坚持原价，此时交易可能陷入僵局；还可以是对对方的还盘进行再还盘。

学习活动2 还盘函识读与撰写

学习目标

1. **知识目标**
   ◆能识读各类还盘函。
   ◆能掌握还盘函的典型句式。

2. **技能目标**
   ◆能掌握商务信函三段式法则并完成还盘函撰写。
   ◆能识别函电中的特殊用语，根据中心词汇准确把握函电意图。
   ◆能够根据客户要求，运用英语灵活处理还盘函中的日常业务。

3. **素养目标**
　　◆通过多样式学习方式提高自主学习能力，增强英语学习兴趣。
　　◆通过情景模拟增强对工作岗位的认知感，提高与国际客户沟通交流的信心。
　　◆通过小组合作增强沟通表达能力，培养团结合作精神，提高工作抗压能力。
4. **思政目标**
　　◆通过邮件内容识别船运公司名称及船籍，增强民族自豪感。

学习课时

14 课时

学习过程

一、识读还盘函－集装箱价格

（1）
From Jennifer Ye
To John Binh—Cargo Connection；antonychen@ cc-cargo connection. com
Sent Monday March 23 2009 8：10 PM
Subject Re：FCL inquiry：Jiangmen to Oklahoma，USA

Dear John
We got COSCO's rate from Jiangmen to OK 74055. It is cheaper and to door service as well，we would like to provide net/net rate as below for your reference：
Carrier：COSCO
POL：Jiangmen
Final destination：OK 74055
VIA：LB
Ocean freight：USD 3 360/20'GP
CY closing：Mon Wed Fri　（feeder）
ETD sat.（HK）
T/T appx 24days
Validity：5th April
Subject to local charges at both ends
Best regards
Jennifer Ye

（2）

From John Binh-Cargo Connection

Sent 2009-03-25 09：12：49

To Jennifer Ye：antonychen @ cc-cargo connection. com

Subject FCL inquiry：Jiangmen to Oklahoma USA

Dear Jennifer,

We note your message and thank you very much for your cooperation.

Please use COSCO service. Hopefully everything is under your control. Please go ahead and arrange the container with Mr. Sam.

Please choose the good container because mosaics brick is very heavy, about 17 500 kgs.

Have a nice day!

Keep us informed of further development.

Best regards

John

【任务要求】请借助网络工具阅读信函，并翻译信函。

【任务分析】

◆Answer the following questions according to the letter.

1. Which carrier does Jennifer recommend for this offer?

_____

_____

2. Why does Jennifer give up Hanjin and take COSCO instead?

_____

_____

3. Compared with Hanjin, is COSCO's rate higher or lower?

_____

_____

4. What is the total weight of the freight?

_____

_____

_____

◆Translate the following sentences into English.

1. 我方现将净运费报价如下，以供参考。

_____

_____

2. 已获悉贵方通知，非常感谢贵司的合作。

_____

_____

3. 希望贵司能够顺利处理一切相关事宜。

_____

_____

4. 请及时告知货物最新状态。

_____

_____

【制订方案】请小组讨论，拟出以上信函的语法知识点和信函大意。

_____

_____

_____

_____

_____

_____

_____

_____

【任务实施】请采用专业角度翻译信函。

信函（一）_____

_____

_____

_____

_____

_____

信函（二）

_____

二、撰写还盘函

【任务要求】撰写报盘函和还盘函。

背景资料：

报价信息如下

承运人：MSK

启运港：Shenzhen

目的港：Los Angeles

海运费：USD1 045/20'GP（比 Hanjin 便宜）

截关日：周一至周三

开船日：周六

航程：大约 16 天

服务：门到门运输服务

报价有效期：12 月 20 日

实训任务：

1. 请以深圳××国际物流公司货代员 Sally 的身份给货代员 Mary 报价；

2. 请以货代员 Mary 的身份回复深圳××国际物流公司货代员 Sally，同意其报价并委托她全程安排此次运输。

【任务分析】请分析并回答以下问题。

1. 翻译背景资料信息：

承运人：MSK _____

启运港：Shenzhen_____

目的港：Los Angeles _____

海运费：USD1 045/20'GP（比 Hanjin 便宜）_____

截关日：周一至周三 _____

开船日：周六 _____

航程：大约 16 天 _____

服务：门到门运输服务 _____

报价有效期：12 月 20 日 _____

2. 翻译：我们现在为你提供另外一家承运人的价格，其更便宜，并且是门到门运输服务。

_____

_____

3. 翻译：某人对……感到满意；安排。

_____

_____

【制订方案】

请小组讨论，根据商务信函三段式法则分别拟出报盘函和还盘函的段落大意。

_____

_____

_____

_____

_____

_____

【任务实施】请根据以上信息，撰写报盘函和还盘函。

三、识读还盘函

【任务要求】请借助网络工具阅读以下信函，并完成以下题目。

Task 1：Exporter's offer

业务背景：海尔集团上海分公司的叶明收到德国博格公司斯蒂文·戴维斯关于 100 台 KFPD-26GW/03ECC12 号海尔空调的询价，要求其报汉堡港到岸价最低价。请以叶明的名义给斯蒂文·戴维斯写一封报价信。

Dear Mr. Davis,

Re：Haier Air Conditioners

Your e-mail of February 11 asking us to offer you the captioned goods has received our immediate attention. We are pleased to know that you are interested in our products.

We take pleasure in making you an offer for Haier air conditioners No. KFRD-26GW/03ECC12 as follows, provided your reply reaches us within 7 days from today：

Unit Price：USD 500 per set CIF Hamburg.

Payment：By confirmed, irrevocable letter of credit payable by draft at sight.

Packing：At buyer's option.

Shipment：To be effected on or before May 31st from Shanghai to Hamburg, allowing partial shipments and transshipment.

Insurance：To be covered by the seller for 110% of the invoice value covering all risks and war risk.

This is an unusual opportunity for you to get an unusual product. I'm looking forward to receiving your initial order as soon as possible.

Yours truly,

Ye Ming

【任务分析】请做好课堂笔记，记录重要语法点知识。

_____

_____

_____

_____

_____

【制订方案】请根据商务信函三段式法则简括信函段落大意。

【任务实施】请小组讨论，并翻译信函。

Task 2：Importer's counter-offer

业务背景：斯蒂文·戴维斯收到叶明的报价函后，觉得价格稍高，希望对方能将价格降低至每台空调 450 美元并将装运期提前到 4 月 30 日之前。请以斯蒂文·戴维斯的名义给叶明写一封还盘函。

Dear Mr. Ye,

Re：Haier air conditioners

We acknowledge with thanks receipt of your offer of February 15 for the subject goods.

In reply, we regret to say that we can't accept it because your price is on the high side. We do not deny that the quality of your product is slightly better, but there should not be such a big gap between your prices and those of other suppliers.

In order to conclude the transaction, we would like to make the following counter-offer: "200 sets Haier air conditioners No. KFRD-26GW/03ECC12, at USD 450 per set CIF Hamburg and shipment is to be effected on or before April 30, other terms as per your e-mail dated February 15."

We hope you can accept the counter-offer and wait for your favorable reply.

Yours truly,

Steven Davis

【任务分析】请做好课堂笔记，记录重要语法点知识。

_____

_____

_____

_____

_____

【制订方案】请根据商务信函三段式法则简括信函段落大意。

_____

_____

_____

_____

_____

【任务实施】请小组讨论，并翻译信函。

_____

_____

学习任务四（1） 还盘函 英文词汇学习

Task 3：集装箱价格

（3）

From：Jennifer Ye

To：John Binh Cargo Connection；antonychen@ cc-cargo connection. com

Sent：Tuesday，March 24，2009 5：30 PM

Subject：Re：FCL inquiry：Jiangmen to Oklahoma，USA

Dear John，

Attached yesterday e-mail is for your reference. We are waiting for so at this time. After checking with shipper, they did not get goods payment from Consignee up to now, so shipper did not send booking to us.

Please note.

Beat regards，

Jennifer

（4）

From：John Binh-Cargo Connection

Sent：March 25，2009 09：40：14

To：Jennifer Ye；antonychen@ cc-cargo connection. com

Subject：Re：FCL inquiry：Jiangmen to Oklahoma，USA Dear，

Dear Jennifer，

Please carry out this shipment, consignee transferred money already. Shipper will receive it within a few days.

Please book and best regards，

John

（5）

From：Jennifer Ye

To：John Binh Cargo Connection；antonychen@ cc-cargo connection. com

Sent：Tuesday，March 24，2009 6:00 PM

Subject：Re：FCL inquiry：Jiangmen to Oklahoma，USA

Dear John，

Well noted.

We sent our booking already，waiting for so now. Kindly await.

Best regards，

Jennifer Ye

【任务要求】请借助网络工具阅读信函，并翻译信函。

【任务分析】

◆Answer the following questions according to the letter.

1. Why has the shipper not sent booking to Jennifer?

_____

_____

2. When will the shipper receive the money?

_____

_____

3. Which carrier do they take for this freight?

_____

_____

4. Has Jennifer received the shipping order yet?

_____

_____

◆Translate the following sentences into English.

1. 经核实，发货人迄今还没有收到买方的货款。

_____

_____

2. 收货人钱已汇出，请尽快执行此次货运。

_____

_____

3. 请根据相关说明和船公司订舱。

_____

_____

4. 我方已把委托书给船公司，正在等船公司放舱。

_____

_____

【制订方案】请小组讨论，拟出以上信函的语法知识点和信函大意。

_____

_____

_____

_____

_____

_____

【任务实施】请翻译以下信函。

信函（三）_____

_____

_____

_____

_____

_____

_____

_____

_____

信函（四）

_____

_____

_____

_____

_____

_____

_____

_____

_____

_____

_____

四、撰写还盘函

【任务要求】撰写还盘函。

背景资料：

香港××物流有限公司委托深圳××国际物流公司向 COSCO 订舱，该批货物重达 18 吨，而 COSCO 仅接受货物为 17.5 吨以下的订舱，否则会要求增收 100 美元的加重费用。

【任务分析】请思考以下问题：

1. 如果要推进该批货物我们该怎么做？作为深圳××国际物流公司你可以给出什么建议？

_____

_____

2. 请将以上建议翻译成英文。

_____

_____

【制订方案】请完成以下问题：

1. 作为香港××物流有限公司员工，我们对该批货物的决策是：

_____

_____

2. 请将以上决策翻译成英文:

_____

_____

【任务实施】请完成以下实训任务:

1. 请以货代员 Sally 身份写邮件给货代员 Marry,让其与收货人协商货物的重量。

_____

_____

_____

_____

_____

_____

_____

_____

_____

2. 请以货代员 Marry 身份回复货代员 Sally 相关信息。

_____

_____

_____

_____

_____

_____

_____

_____

学习任务五　信息变更函

工作情境描述

Joey 在深圳某货运代理公司客服人员岗位，经过为期两周的岗位工作，他渐渐对业务熟悉了，但今天又出现了新的问题，客户要求变更信息：

在前期函电中，由于货物超重由 COSCO 船运公司更改为 MSK 船运公司，货代员 John 抱怨重量计算错误，导致本次货运成本增高……

同时印度代理指示国内代理订万海直航船，安排货物灯具从深圳港到印度的钦奈港的运输。但由于万海的直航船已爆舱，Jennifer 只好告知印度代理，并提供另外两种可选择的方案……

代理 Sara 报价给代理 Heidi，安排货物从深圳空运到厄瓜多尔的瓜亚基尔。但代理 Heidi 对费用表示疑问……

学习任务解析

学习任务见图 5-1。

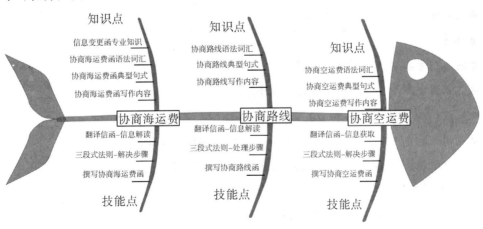

图 5-1　学习任务

20 课时

学习活动 1　协商海运费

学习活动 2　协商路线

学习活动 3　协商空运费

学习活动 1　协商海运费

1. **知识目标**

　　◆能熟记国际货代业务中涉及的专业术语。

　　◆能总结归纳信息变更函类别。

　　◆能充分理解协商海运费函的写作内容。

　　◆能熟记协商海运费的基本词汇。

2. **技能目标**

　　◆能熟练掌握商务信函三段式法则。

　　◆能熟练使用电脑，熟悉常用操作软件。

　　◆能认识并准确运用各种贸易术语和条款。

　　◆能识别函电中的特殊用语，根据中心词汇准确把握函电意图。

　　◆能够根据客户要求，运用英语灵活处理协商海运费中的日常业务。

3. **素养目标**

　　◆通过情景模拟增强对工作岗位的认知感。

　　◆通过角色扮演及业务分析，提升工作岗位应变能力。

◆通过多样化学习方式提高自主学习能力，增强英语学习兴趣。

◆通过小组合作增强沟通表达能力，提高与国际客户沟通交流的信心。

4. 思政目标

◆通过不断的训练和中国礼仪的熏陶，提升商务礼仪认知。

学习课时

8 课时

学习过程

一、总结归纳信息变更函类别

【任务要求】请列出信息更改函的更改内容。

_____

_____

_____

_____

总结归纳：

_____

_____

_____

_____

_____

_____

_____

二、理解信息变更函的写作内容

【任务要求】请复述信息变更函的段落大意。

_____

_____

_____

_____

_____

三、识读信息变更函－协商海运费

（1）

From：John Binh-Cargo Connection

Sent：2009-03-31 08：04：36

To：Maggielin@ cc-cargo connection. com；Jennifer Ye；

Subject：Re FCL inquiry：Jiangmen to Oklahoma，USA

Dear Jennifer and Maggie，

You might understand the wrong calculation of gross weight for shipment. This is the biggest mistake from the shipper. This caused a wrong routing and a lot of extra cost. Routing is from Jiangmen to Dallas instead of going to consignee door with COSCO service 17. 2 tons.

Actual weight is now 17 tons. Give us a favor, please discuss with MSK our cargo is now 17 tons, ask them to keep the price same as COSCO to OK 74055.

If MSK reject to move the freight to OK 74055, ask to reduce the ocean freight because our cargo is less than our forecast. You also know how expensive inland trucking from Dallas to OK 74055.

The shipper made us crazy, changed everything, loss money.

Look forward to hearing from you.

Thanks a lot and best regards，

John

（2）

From：Jennifer Ye

To：Maggielin@ cc-cargo connection. com；Jennifer Ye；

Sent：Monday, March 30, 2009 6:54 PM

Subject：Re FCL inquiry：Jiangmen to Oklahoma, USA

Dear John,

We fully understood the situation of this shipment.

After hard negotiation with MSK, they advised that their rate based on goods weight under 18T.

In other word, the rate same, either 17. 5T or 17T.

We have no alternative but keep the original ocean freight we offered. Kindly understand.

Best regards,

Jennifer Ye

【任务要求】请借助网络工具阅读信函，并翻译信函。

【任务分析】

◆Answer the following questions according to the letter.

1. What is the actual weight of the goods finally?

_____

_____

2. Who makes the mistake of weight according to John?

_____

_____

3. What does John ask Jennifer to do from MSK?

_____

_____

4. What's the alternative John requires from MSK?

_____

_____

5. What is MSK's rule on rate?

_____

_____

◆Complete the blanks according to the information given below.

John informs that the shipper made a mistake about the calculation of 1. _____ for the shipment, and it led to a wrong 2. _____ and more 3. _____. John hopes that MSK can transport their cargos to 4. _____ instead of 5. _____, and he hopes MSK can keep the price the same as COSCO. If not, they hope MSK can cut down the 6. _____.

【制订方案】请小组讨论，拟出以上信函的语法知识点。

_____

_____

_____

_____

_____

_____

_____

_____

【任务实施】请翻译信函。

信函（一）_____

_____

_____

_____

_____

_____

_____

_____

_____

_____

信函（二）_____

_____

_____

_____

_____

_____

_____

_____

_____

_____

_____

_____

学习任务五（1）　信息变更函 英文词汇学习

【任务要求】请借助网络工具阅读以下信函，并翻译信函。

Requesting to Advance the Shipment

业务背景：上海天美纺织品有限公司向法国海斯顿纺织品公司订购了一批桌布，订单号为954，原计划 5 月份装货，现请以上海天美公司为名写信要求提早装运。

From：Shanghai Tianmei Textile Co.，LTD.

To：Heston Textile Company of France.

Re：Requesting to Advance the Shipment.

Dear Sirs，

We refer to our purchase contract No. 954. Under the terms of the contract，delivery is scheduled for May 2021 by ship. We would like to bring delivery forward to April 2021 now.

We realize that the change of delivery date will probably inconvenience you and we offer our sincere apologies. We know that you will understand that we would not ask for earlier delivery if we did not have compelling reasons for doing so. And we have learned from the carrier that they can

offer free storage for one day and $ 0.05 per kg for the second day onwards with the minimum charge of $ 50 per day. Please confirm for us. Thanks.

In view of our longstanding, cordial commercial relationship, we would be very grateful if you would make a special effort to comply with our request. We look forward to your early reply.

Yours faithfully,

John

【任务分析】

◆Answer the following questions according to the letter in English.

1. Mode of transportation:

2. Name of commodity:

3. Country of origin (goods):

4. Country of destination:

5. Port of loading:

6. Port of transshipment:

7. Original month of loading:

8. Subject of the letter:

9. Shipper:

10. Consignee:

【制订方案】请小组讨论，拟出以上信函的语法知识点并选取典型句式造句。

_____

_____

_____

_____

_____

_____

_____

【任务实施】请翻译信函。

_____

_____

_____

_____

_____

_____

_____

_____

_____

_____

_____

_____

_____

四、撰写信息变更函

【任务要求】撰写信息变更函。

背景资料：

货代员 Mary 接到一项业务，向深圳新世纪物流公司 Sally 咨询费用，货物信息如下：

运输方式：空运

启运港：洛杉矶

目的港：深圳

目的地：东莞、中山

货物：水龙头

重量：1 500 千克

预计装货期：7 月份

深圳新世纪物流公司 Sally 早前已经为其报价，但由于重量计算错误特再次提供以下报价信息：

机场提货费：最少 65 美元或 0.05 美元/千克

机场杂费：实报实销（在机场提货超过 3 小时，每小时收 40 美元）

本地费用：深圳到东莞 161 美元，深圳到中山 180 美元

仓储费（如需要）：免堆一天，第二天起每天最低 20 美元或者 0.02 美元/千克

装货期可否提前至 6 月份？

实训任务：

请以货代员 Sally 身份向对方更新报价内容，信函除了需涵盖所有报价信息外，还需详述货物信息内容。

【任务分析】请分析并回答以下问题。

1. 翻译货物信息：

_____

_____

_____

_____

_____

2. 翻译报价信息：

_____

_____

_____

_____

_____

_____

【制订方案】

请小组讨论，根据商务信函三段式法则分别拟出信函的段落大意。

_____

_____

_____

_____

_____

_____

_____

【任务实施】请根据以上信息，撰写信函。

学习活动 2　协商路线

学习目标

1. **知识目标**
   ◆能充分理解协商路线函的写作内容。
   ◆能熟记协商路线函的基本词汇。
2. **技能目标**
   ◆能识别函电中的特殊用语，根据中心词汇准确把握函电意图。
   ◆能够根据客户要求，运用英语灵活处理协商路线函中的日常业务。
3. **素养目标**
   ◆通过各种学习工具提高自主学习能力，增强英语学习兴趣。
   ◆通过情景模拟增强对工作岗位的认知感，提高与国际客户沟通交流的信心。
   ◆通过小组合作增强沟通表达能力，培养团结合作精神，提高工作抗压能力。

学习课时

8 课时

学习过程

一、识读信息变更函 - 协商路线

（1）
To：Skyline Shipping & Logistics；Francis；Fanny；Heidi
Sent：Thursday, February 19, 2009 7：04 AM
Subject：Re：Nomination-arka Leisure & Entertainments Pvt, Ltd

Dear Muurthy,
WHL informed that they can not release so to as there are too many booking orders for direct

line. At this stage, we have two suggestions as below:
Choose transshipment of WHL via port Klang
Ocean freight: USD54/40'HQ
CY closing: Mon
ETD: Wed
T/T: appx. 13days
Max goods weight: under25T
Validity: 28.02.09
Remark: 14 days free detention at final destination
Choose another direct line
Carrier: K-Line
Ocean freight: USD560/40HQ
CY closing: Wed
ETD: Fri
T/T: appx. 10days
Maxgoods weight: under 25T
Validity: 28.02.09
Remark: 14 days free detention at final destination
Subject to local charges at both ends
We are waiting for your decision to follow up.
Best regards,
Jennifer Ye

---

(2)
From: Skyline Shipping & Logistics
Sent: 2009-02-19 15:50:20
To: Jennifer Ye; Francis; Fanny ; Heidi
Subject: Re: Nomination-arka Leisure & Entertainments Pvt, Ltd

Dear Jennifer Ye,
Please go ahead with WHL via port Klang.
Please advise us the vessel schedule
Regards,
G. K. Muurthy

(3)

From：Jennifer Ye

Sent：Thursday，February 19，2009 5:24 PM

To：Skyline Shipping & Logistics；Francis；Fanny；Heidi

Subject：Re：Nomination-arka Leisure & Entertainments Pvt，Ltd

Dear Muurthy,

Well noted and we will arrange your goods via port Klang to chennal. But contacted shipper just now, Kevin（shipper）advised that there are some problems of customs clearance documents, so they cannot catch the vessel on next Monday. If you choose WHL, we have to postpone this shipment to March and we will update our rate of March next week. Kindly note. Waiting for your comments. Thanks.

Best regards,

Jennifer Ye

【任务要求】请借助网络工具阅读信函，并翻译信函。

【任务分析】

◆按要求记录重点词汇和语法知识点。

◆Answer the following questions according to the letter.

1. Why can't WHL release so?

_____

_____

2. What alternatives does Jennifer provide to deal with the problem of so?

_____

_____

3. Which suggestion does Muurthy take?

_____

_____

4. If Muurthy takes WHL, what problems can be produced?

_____

_____

◆Translate the following sentences into English.

1. 直线航班已经爆满。

_____

_____

2. 目的港可以 14 天免费用箱。

_____

_____

3. 由于报关单据问题，发货人赶不上此次班轮。

_____

_____

4. 此次货运日期将推迟至五月，稍后我们会告知贵方相关最新消息。

_____

_____

5. 起运港没有足够的货柜。

_____

_____

【任务实施】请翻译第 1 篇和第 3 篇信函。

学习任务五（2）协商路线 英文词汇学习

二、撰写信息变更函 – 协商路线

【任务要求】撰写信息变更函。

背景资料：

深圳××物流有限公司货代员 Sally 告知香港××物流有限公司货代员 Mary，由于疫情原因 APL 直航的订舱爆满，深圳港没有充足的货柜，船公司不能予以放舱。

实训任务：

1. 请以货代员 Sally 身份写邮件给 Mary，内容涵盖以上信息，并给予建议。

2. 请以货代员 Mary 身份回复与收货人协商后的结果。

【任务分析】作为货代员 Sally 可以给出哪些建议？并将其翻译成英文。

_____

_____

_____

【制订方案】请小组讨论根据商务信函三段式法则分别拟出信函的段落大意。

_____

_____

_____

_____

_____

_____

_____

_____

【任务化解】请小组讨论根据段落大意拟出相应的典型句式。

1. 表达_____句式：

_____

_____

_____

2. 表达_____句式：

_____

_____

_____

3. _____句式：

_____

_____

_____

【任务实施】请根据以上信息，撰写信函。

_____

_____

_____

_____

_____

_____

_____

_____

_____

_____

_____

_____

_____

_____

_____

学习任务五（3）　典型句式 英文词汇学习

学习活动 3　协商空运费

工作情境描述

　　香港××物流有限公司 Mary 致函深圳××国际物流有限公司 Sally，询问从深圳到孟买（Mumbai）29 千克的空运费。

　　Sally 告知国泰航空（CA）每千克 2.7 美元，按 45 千克起算；TG 航空每千克 2.4 美元，按 100 千克起算；订舱时，请再次确认价格和舱位。由于货轻，建议走快递，每千克 5.1 美元。

学习目标

1. **知识目标**
　　◆能充分理解协商空运费函的写作内容。
　　◆能熟记协商空运费函的基本词汇。
2. **技能目标**
　　◆能熟练掌握商务信函三段式法则。
　　◆能识别函电中的特殊用语，根据中心词汇准确把握函电意图。
　　◆能够根据客户要求，运用英语灵活处理协商空运费函中的日常业务。
3. **素养目标**
　　◆通过各种学习工具提高自主学习能力，增强英语学习兴趣。
　　◆通过情景模拟增强对工作岗位的认知感，提高与国际客户沟通交流的信心。
　　◆通过小组合作增强沟通表达能力，培养团结合作精神，提高工作抗压能力。

学习课时

　　4 课时

学习过程

一、识读信息变更函 - 协商空运费

（1）

From：Heidi Ma

Sent：2011-08-12 11:04:26

To：Sarachen@ cc-cargo connection. com

Subject：Air freight enquiry to Guayaquil

Dear Sara,

Please quote air freight for below shipment from Shenzhen to Guayaquil, thank you.

2BOXES

435X215X85mm

Weight 30 KLS（total）

Computers parts/Accessories

Regards,

Heidi Ma

（2）

From：Saracen

To：Heidi Ma

Sent：Monday August 15, 2011 9:50 AM

Subject：Re：Air freight enquiry to Guayaquil

Dear Heidi,

Please refer to below air freight rates to Guayaquil

A/F：+45kg：rmb58/kg +handling：rmb150

Airline：E6（Deliver goods to Shenzhen warehouse, fly from HKG）

（HKG- ANC-... -GYE）

Frequency：Daily

Transit Time：about 7-10 days

Valid：19 Aug.（please recheck with us about the rate and space whilebooking）

A/F：+100kg：rmb58/kg

Airline: UPS

Via MIA

Frequency: Daily

Transit Time: about 10 days

Valid: 19 Aug. (please recheck with us one time while booking)

Kindly note that the above rates should be subject to local charges at both sides.

Should you have any questions, please don't hesitate to contact us.

Thanks.

Best regards.

Saracen

Marketing department

---

(3)

From: Heidi Ma

Sent: 2011-08-15 11:42:39

To: Sarachen

Subject: Air freight enquiry to Guayaquil

Is 30kgs charged as 45/100?

---

(4)

From: Saracen

To: Heidi Ma

Sent: Monday August 15, 2011 11:46 AM

Subject: Re: Air freight enquiry to Guayaquil

Dear: Heidi Ma,

It is calculated based on 45kgs/100kgs.

Should you have any questions, please don't hesitate to contact us.

Thanks.

Best regards,

Sachem

（5）

From：Heidi Ma

Sent：2011-08-15 11：49：09

To：Sarachen

Subject：Air freight enquiry to Guayaquil

As there is too much kilogram difference, is it possible not to be charged as 45/200? Besides, can you handle the cargo ex Shenzhen?

（6）

From：Saracen

To：Heidi Ma

Sent：Monday August 15, 2011 11：58 AM

Subject：Re：Air freight enquiry to Guayaquil

Dear Heidi,

1. Weight is 36kgs, yet the two airliners calculate based on 45kgs/100kgs. Any cargo below 45kgs/100kgs is based on the standard. Suggest taking E6.

2. Weight can handle cargos ex Shenzhen.

Should you have any questions, please don't hesitate to contact us.

Thanks.

Best regards,

Saracen

Marketing department

2011-08-15

【任务要求】请借助网络工具阅读信函，并翻译信函。

【任务分析】

◆按要求记录难点词汇。

_____

_____

_____

_____

◆Answer the following questions according to the letter.

1. Suppose you were Heidi, which airliner will you take for the shipment? And why?

2. What are the air rates of E6 and UPS respectively for the shipment?

3. Why does Sara emphasize "recheck with us about the rate and space while booking"?

4. In what way does Heidi want the cargo calculated?

◆Translate the following sentences into English.

1. 收费按 45 千克起算。

2. 如果货重 45 千克以下, 航空公司收费按 45 千克起算。

3. 建议走 E6。

4. 我们接深圳出的货。

【任务实施】请翻译第 2 篇和第 6 篇信函。

学习任务五（4）协商空运费 英文词汇学习

二、撰写信息变更函 – 协商空运费

【任务要求】撰写信息变更函。

背景资料：（工作情境描述）

实训任务：

请以货代员 Sally 身份写信回复货代员 Mary，内容涵盖以上背景资料中的要点。

【制订方案】请小组讨论根据商务信函三段式法则分别拟出信函的段落大意。

【任务化解】请小组讨论根据段落大意拟出相应的典型句式。

1. 表达_____句式：

_____

_____

2. 表达_____句式：

_____

_____

3. _____句式：

_____

_____

【任务实施】请根据以上信息，撰写信函。

_____

_____

_____

_____

_____

_____

_____

_____

_____

_____

_____

_____

学习任务五（5）协商空运费函典型句式 英文词汇学习

学习任务六　达成协议函

Joey 在深圳某货运代理公司客服人员岗位，随着业务的进展，正与客户达成交易过程中，需要通过洽谈与客户达成最终的业务协议。

学习任务见图6-1。

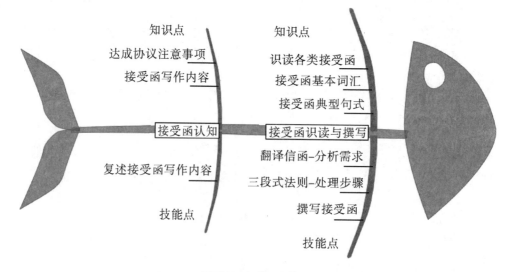

图6-1　学习任务

建议课时

16 课时

工作流程与活动

学习活动 1　接受函认知
学习活动 2　接受函识读与撰写

学习活动 1　接受函认知

学习目标

1. **知识目标**

　◆能熟记达成协议前应注意的问题。

　◆能理解接受函的写作内容。

2. **技能目标**

　◆能复述接受函写作内容。

3. **素养目标**

　◆通过小组合作增强沟通能力，提高与国际客户沟通交流的信心。

　◆通过角色扮演及业务分析，提升工作岗位应变能力。

4. **思政目标**

　◆通过询盘函发信主体，强调中国国际地位的不断提升，增强民族自豪感。

学习课时

4 课时

学习过程

一、接受函相关知识

【任务要求】请列出达成协议前应注意的问题。

_____

_____

_____

_____

_____

_____

_____

_____

_____

_____

知识链接

　　一个完整的进出口贸易合同，一般包含有五个方面的内容：①关于货物本身的内容；②关于货物运输的内容；③关于货物保险的内容；④关于货款结算的内容；⑤万一合同在履行过程中买卖双方发生疑义、异议或纠纷，应采取什么方法解决。

　　达成协议函亦称为接受函，是达成交易和订立合同必不可少的环节。接受在法律上叫做承诺，是指受盘人在发盘有效期内完全同意发盘的全部内容，愿意订立合同的一种表示。

　　在达成协议前应注意以下问题：

　　1. 明确交易各方具体的名称、地址、联系方式等；

　　2. 交易对方主体资信的调查了解（注册地、资产、实际管理机构等信息）；

　　3. 合同标的货物描述及规范（是否有质量标准）；

　　4. 明确具体的交货时间；

　　5. 产品不合格的索赔时效（收货后几天）；

6. 定金和预付款;

7. 合同的完整性;

8. 收汇不着的风险;

9. 合同生效及自动续展约定;

10. 合同终止、解除条件及赔偿、补偿等事项的约定;

11. 合同争议的解决。

二、接受函写作内容

【任务要求】请复述接受函写作内容。

_____

_____

_____

_____

_____

_____

_____

_____

_____

【任务要求】请复述确认函写作内容。

_____

_____

_____

_____

_____

_____

_____

_____

学习活动2　接受函识读与撰写

学习目标

1. **知识目标**
   ◆能熟记国际货代达成协议业务中涉及的专业术语。
   ◆能熟记询盘函的基本词汇。
   ◆能识读各类接受函。
   ◆能掌握接受函的典型句式。

2. **技能目标**
   ◆能熟练掌握商务信函三段式法则。
   ◆能熟练使用电脑，熟悉常用操作软件。
   ◆能识别函电中的特殊用语，根据中心词汇准确把握函电意图。
   ◆能够根据客户要求，运用英语灵活处理接受函中的日常业务。

3. **素养目标**
   ◆通过情景模拟增强对工作岗位的认知感。
   ◆通过角色扮演及业务分析，提升工作岗位应变能力。
   ◆通过多样化学习方式提高自主学习能力，增强英语学习兴趣。
   ◆通过小组合作增强沟通表达能力，提高与国际客户沟通交流的信心。

学习课时

12 课时

学习过程

一、识读接受函－广东至俄克拉荷马

（1）

From：John Binh-Cargo Connection

Sent：2009-03-31 11：01：29

To：Jennifer Ye：maggielin@ cc-cargo connection. com：

Subject：Re：FCL inquiry：Jiangmen to Oklahoma，USA

Dear Jennifer，

Is there any change in routing? If no，please send details to MSK for issuing MBL. HBL is also enclosed for your reference and AMS filing. Please forward it to MSK also. If you have any question，feel free to contact us.

Best regards，

John

（2）

From：Jennifer Ye

Sent：2009-03-31 11：49：59

To：John Binh-Cargo Connection：maggielin@ cc-cargo connection. com

Subject：Re：FCL inquiry：Jiangmen to Oklahoma，USA

Dear John，

There is not any change inrouting. Maggie will follow up your instruction of BL. Please note.

Best regards，

Jennifer Ye

【任务要求】请借助网络工具阅读信函，并翻译信函。

【任务分析】

◆按要求记录重点词汇。

_____

_____

_____

_____
_____
_____
_____
_____

◆Complete the blanks according to the information given below.

John requests Jennifer to send detailed information to 1. _____ to issue 2. _____ if there is no change in routing, and encloses 3. _____ for her reference and AMS filing. After checking, Jennifer informs John that there is no 4. _____ and Maggie will track the instruction of 5. _____.

◆Translate the following sentences into English.

1. 请告知运输路线是否有变动？

_____
_____

2. 如果确认无误，请提供相关提单资料给马士基船运公司进行订舱。

_____
_____

3. 如有问题，请随时联系我们。

_____
_____

4. 随信附上货代提单，供您参阅。

_____
_____

5. 运输路线没有任何变动，我会一直跟踪这批货。

_____
_____

【任务实施】请翻译信函。

_____
_____
_____

_____

_____

_____

_____

_____

_____

_____

_____

学习任务六（1） 接受函 英文词汇学习

二、撰写接受函

【任务要求】撰写接受函。

背景资料：

货代员 Mary 致函深圳××国际物流公司货代员 Sally，表示同意其向 MSK 公司订舱，并请 Sally 将详细资料按要求提交 MSK 船公司申报 AMS 及签发主提单。

实训任务：

请以货代员 Mary 身份写邮件给货代员 Sally 告知上述内容。

【制订方案】请小组讨论根据商务信函三段式法则分别拟出信函的段落大意。

_____

_____

_____

【任务化解】请小组讨论根据段落大意拟出相应的典型句式。

1. 表达_____句式：

_____

_____

_____

2. 表达_____句式：

_____
_____
_____

3. _____句式：

_____
_____
_____

【任务实施】请根据以上信息，撰写信函。

_____
_____
_____
_____
_____
_____
_____
_____
_____
_____
_____
_____
_____
_____
_____
_____
_____
_____

三、识读接受函－缩略词

【任务要求】请借助网络工具阅读以下信函，并翻译信函。

FM：Sha Holly

TO：ATL Chris

July 17

Booking Advice

Re New Bkg Fr Cato Fob Qingdao To Clt

Vndr	Po#	Sty#	Ctns	Pcs	Description	l/c#	Kgs	Cbms	Rdy
G-HI	12402	W2600500	31.25	250	leather coats	A960165	595	2.76	7/23

（China 13511

Tushu）

Total 1251，0002，37511.14

G-M 12371

Shantung （omitted）

Total 125　　1 000　　2 750　　11.59

Plan to combine above cargo in 1 x 20 * to ship on nyk fdr "sea bright v. 9635" slg qin 7/26, cnctg main vsl "california zues v. 69" with etd kobe 8/2, eta lax 8/13. pls adv. thks & rgds.

Fm Atl To Sha

Rea client name booking fob qin … cnee confirm ok to combine po# 12402, 13511-2 with po # 12371-3 for total 22.73 cbms to shp in 1 x20' via mini land bridge vsl. However cnee advd they really need a mlb vsl with earlier eta than calif. Zues v. 69. pls ck with other mlb carriers n adv if any will have a vsl with earlier eta clt … if not, cnee adv ok to shp as you mentioned above.

Fm Sha To Atl

Rea client name bkg/fob qin … nyk "calif. Zues v. 69" sld qin 7/26 is the fastest vsl we can find. So wil book space on this Vsl.

Fm Atl To Sha

Ok to ship via calif. Zues as plnd.

【任务分析】

◆Explain these abbreviations or codes in English and Chinese.

1. CLT：

2. VNDR：

3. CTNS：

4. RDY：

5. SLG：

6. VSL：

7. LAX：

8. CNEE：

9. MLB：

10. PO：

11. SHP：

12. ADVA：

13. CK：

14. PLND：

◆Please transfer these letters into lower case with electronic copy.

◆Regarding this shipment, fill in the blanks based on above mails.

1. mode of transportation：

2. name of commodity：

3. country of origin：

4. country of destination：

5. port of loading：

6. port of transhipment：

7. carrier：

8. ETD：

9. port of discharge：

10. ETA：

11. shipper on MBL：

12. location of marker/factory：

13. cargo volume：

14. total CBM：

15. subject of the letter：

【任务实施】请翻译信函。

四、识读接受函

---

(3)

From：Maggielin

To：Jennifer Ye；John Binh Cargo Connection；antonychen@ cc-cargo connection. co

Sent：Tuesday, March 31, 2009 9:39 AM

Subject：Re：FCL inquiry：Jiangmen to Oklahoma, USA

Dear John,

I found some difference on consignee's company name between the shipper's shipping instruction and your HB/L. Is HB/L OK already?

Can I use your HB/L's information to fill in AMS? And send MB/L's information to carrier?

Please reconfirm, thanks！

Best regards,

Maggie Lin

---

(4)

From；John Binh-Cargo Connection

Sent；2009-04-01 08:04:33

To：Maggielin@ cc-cargo connection. com

Subject：Re：FCL inquiry：Jiangmen to Oklahoma, USA

Dear Maggie,

Please send MBL and debit note once available.

Thanks and regards,

John

---

(5)

From：Jennifer Ye

To：John Binh- Cargo Connection；@ cc-cargo connection. com；antonychen@ cc-cargo connection. co

Sent：Tuesday, march31, 2009 5:45 PM

Subject：Re：FCL inquiry：Jiangmen to Oklahoma, USA

Dear John,

Please advise profit share of this shipment. Thanks.

Best regards,

Jennifer Ye

（6）

From：John Binh- Cargo Connection

Sent：2009-04-01 10:48:57

To：Jennifer Ye；maggielin@cc-cargo connection.com

Subject：Re：FCL inquiry：Jiangmen to Oklahoma, USA

Dear Jennifer,

Finally, San agreed to pay USD 100. She needs invoice from you.

So, profit share is USD 50 for each party.

Please send us your debit note USD2 800-USD50＝USD2 750.

Please arrange Telex release for MBL. We will arrange the wire transfer soon.

Any questions, feel free to contact us.

Best regards,

John

（7）

From：Jennifer Ye

To：John Binh- Cargo Connection；@cc-cargo connection.com；antonychen@cc-cargo connection.co

Sent：Tuesday, march31, 2009 10:43 PM

Subject：Re：FCL inquiry：Jiangmento Oklahoma, USA

Dear John：

Noted with thanks.

Maggie will send debit note to you soon.

Best regards,

Jennifer Ye

（8）

From：John Binh- Cargo Connection

Sent：2009-04-29 09:15:41

To：Jennifer Ye；maggielin@cc-cargo connection.com

Subject：Re：FCL inquiry：Jiangmen to Oklahoma, USA

Dear Jennifer,

Container arrived in USA safely and delivered to consignee door.

Thank you.

Best regards,

John

【任务要求】请借助网络工具阅读信函，并翻译指定内容。

【任务分析】

◆按要求记录重点词汇。

_____

_____

_____

_____

_____

_____

◆Answer the following questions according to the letter.

1. What is the purpose of the letter?

_____

_____

2. What information will have to be confirmed in the letter?

_____

_____

3. Which document will be based on if there is some disagreement between HBL and shipping instructions?

_____

_____

4. Who will issue MBL? What about debit note?

_____

_____

5. What's the profit share of this forwarding for each party?

_____

_____

6. Why is the debit note USD 2 750?

_____

_____

7. In what way will John get the MBL?

_____

_____

8. How long does the shipment approximately take from the shipper to the consignee?

_____

_____

◆Complete the blanks according to the information given below.

Maggie informs John that there is difference on the consignee's company name between the _____ and the _____ . And she asks if she could use the _____ information to fill in AMS, and send _____ information to the carrier.

Jennifer requests John to inform her of _____ of this shipment.

John advises Jennifer that the profit share is _____ for each party, and requests her to send them the _____ USD 2 750 and arrange _____ for MBL, then John will arrange the _____ . In the end, John advises Jennifer that the _____ has safely delivered to the consignee's _____ .

【任务实施】请翻译指定内容。

_____

_____

_____

_____

_____

_____

_____

_____

_____

_____

_____

学习任务六（2）接受函 英文词汇学习

五、撰写接受函

【任务要求】撰写接受函。

背景资料：

香港××物流有限公司 Mary 决定所有信息以货代提单资料为准，并该批货物的利润分成是各方 70 美元，账单为 930 美元。同时请求安排货主提单。

实训任务：

1. 请以香港××物流有限公司 Mary 身份写邮件给深圳××物流公司 Sally，告知背景资料信息。

2. 请深圳××物流公司 Sally 身份回复上述邮件，并告知集装箱已安全抵达美国并送至收货人。

【制订方案】请小组讨论根据商务信函三段式法则分别拟出信函的段落大意。

_____

_____

_____

_____

_____

_____

【任务实施】请根据以上信息，撰写信函。

_____

_____

学习任务七　投诉函、索赔函、理赔函

工作情境描述

Joey 任职于深圳某货运代理公司客服人员岗位，近期收到了客户发来的投诉索赔函，正在读取并拟稿回函……

学习任务解析

学习任务见图 7-1。

图 7-1　学习任务

建议课时

20 课时

工作流程与活动

学习活动 1　投诉函、索赔函、理赔函认知
学习活动 2　投诉函、索赔函识读与撰写
学习活动 3　理赔函识读与撰写

学习活动 1　投诉函、索赔函、理赔函认知

学习目标

1. **知识目标**
   ◆能理解投诉、索赔和理赔的相关知识。
   ◆能了解投诉、索赔和理赔的语言特点。
2. **技能目标**
   ◆能熟记投诉函、索赔函常用句式。
   ◆能熟记投诉函、索赔函的写作内容。
3. **素养目标**
   ◆通过多样化学习方式提高自主学习能力，增强英语学习兴趣。
   ◆通过小组合作增强沟通能力，提高与国际客户沟通交流的信心。
4. **思政目标**
   ◆通过角色扮演和中国礼仪的熏陶，提升处理商务投诉索赔的能力。

2 课时

一、投诉、索赔与理赔

【任务要求】学习投诉、索赔及理赔的相关知识，并补充空白处内容。

1. 索赔（claim）

索赔是指在国际贸易中，签订合同的双方有一方违反合同的规定，给另一方造成损失，损失的一方根据合同规定向违约方提出赔偿损失的要求。

属于卖方责任而引起买方索赔的主要有：_____

_____

属于买方责任而引起卖方索赔的有：_____

_____

索赔的依据包括两个方面：（1）法律依据：_____；

（2）事实依据：_____。

2. 理赔（settlement）

理赔是指违约方对遭受损失的一方提出要求赔付金额或实物，承担有关修理、加工整理等费用，或同意换货等索赔要求进行处理的行为。索赔和理赔是一个问题的两个方面，是一项政策性、技术性很强的涉外工作，必须严肃对待和认真处理。

3. 仲裁（arbitration）

仲裁又称公断，是指买卖双方在争议发生之前或之后，签订书面协议，自愿将争议提交双方所同意的第三者予以裁决，以解决争议的一种方式。由于仲裁是依照法律所允许的仲裁程度裁定争端，因而仲裁具有法律约束力，当事人双方必须遵照执行。

4. 不可抗力（force majeure）

不可抗力又称人力不可抗拒，是指在货物买卖合同签订以后，不是订约者任何一方当事人的过失或疏忽，而是发生了当事人不能预见和预防，又无法避免和克服的意外事故，以致不能履行或不能如期履行合同，遭受意外事故的一方，可以免除履行合同的责任或延期履行合同。

Review：

1. 索赔（claim）是指在_____中，签订合同的双方_____，给另一方造成损失，_____根据合同规定向违约方提出赔偿损失的要求。

2. 理赔（settlement）是指违约方对_____提出要求赔付金额或实物，承担有关_____等费用，或同意换货等索赔要求进行_____的行为。

3. 仲裁（arbitration）是指买卖双方在争议发生_____，签订书面协议，自愿将争议提交双方所同意的_____，以解决争议的一种方式。

4. 不可抗力（force majeure）是指在货物买卖合同签订以后，不是订约者任何一方当事人的过失或疏忽，_____，又无法避免和克服的意外事故，_____，遭受意外事故的一方，可以免除履行合同的责任或延期履行合同。

【任务要求】学习投诉、索赔函中的语言特点。

_____

_____

_____

_____

_____

_____

【任务要求】学习投诉函、索赔函语句。

1. We are writing for a replacement of the dictionary included.

_____

2. Would you please correct your shipment by sending the order No. 2 530 by the first available vessel.

_____

3. It would be highly appreciated if you could look into the personal computers, which should have reached our destination two weeks ago.

_____

4. On comparing the goods received with the sample supplied, we were sorry to notice the great differences in the designs of the machines.

5. We feel it necessary to inform you that your last delivery of our order is not up to the usual standard.

6. Upon inspection, it was found that the total content had been short-delivered by 1.5 tons.

7. After having the boxes examined we found that they were not strong enough for long distance delivery.

8. It is regrettable to see that the chemical content of item 022 is not up to the percentage contracted.

9. There is a discrepancy in colors between the received materials and the samples.

10. While placing our order we emphasized that any delay in delivery would definitely add to the cost of the goods. That is why we have to raise a claim on refunds for the loss incurred.

【任务要求】学习索赔函的写作内容。

学习活动 2　投诉函、索赔函识读与撰写

学习目标

1. **知识目标**
   ◆能熟记投诉函、索赔函的基本词汇。
   ◆能掌握投诉函、索赔函的典型句式。

2. **技能目标**
   ◆能熟练掌握商务信函三段式法则。
   ◆能识读函电中的特殊用语，根据中心词汇准确把握函电意图。
   ◆能够根据工作情境，运用英语灵活处理索赔函中的日常业务。

3. **素养目标**
   ◆通过各种学习工具提高自主学习能力，增强英语学习兴趣。
   ◆通过情景模拟增强对工作岗位的认知感，提高与国际客户沟通交流的信心。
   ◆通过小组合作增强沟通表达能力，培养团结合作精神，提高工作抗压能力。

学习课时

10 课时

学习过程

一、识读投诉函、索赔函

【任务要求】学习以下投诉函、索赔函，并完成相应任务。

Dear Mr. Clare,

Our consignee has received the 50 pieces of **printed cotton cloth** which we shipped on March 25.

On **examination** the consignee finds that he still hasn't received the **original customs clearance documents** at this moment. You can use **the tracking number** to check online. As the container has been **docked** for days, this will **incur additional** late fees. In the end, this will **lead to** an increase in the cost of goods for the consignee.

The consignee was very angry. We are therefore writing to inform you these **circumstances**. We hope that this matter can be **resolved** as soon as possible.

Yours faithfully,

Zhejiang Baiyun Garments Co., Ltd.

Li Xin

Sales Manager

【任务分析】

◆按要求记录重点词汇。

_____

_____

_____

_____

_____

_____

_____

_____

【任务实施】请翻译信函。

_____

_____

_____

_____

_____

_____

_____

_____

_____

_____

_____

_____

_____

_____

_____

_____

_____

学习任务七（1）索赔函 英文词汇学习

二、撰写投诉函、索赔函

【任务要求】撰写索赔函。

背景资料：

福建省××股份有限公司于 2021 年 11 月 20 日委托××国际货运代理有限公司承运活性炭（activated carbon）从福州市江阴港运至巴西桑托斯（Santos Brazil），提单号 MSCUFI131，船名航次 Crusader-HK517A。但拖车在×××市至江阴市运输途中发生追尾事故（car crash、rear-end collision），导致集装箱箱体损坏，经第三方现场开箱检查，发现货物破损 6 包，并由此产生以下的费用损失：

1. 货物直接损失：1 200 元（6 包×200 元/包）。

2. 紧急调运货物补缺运费：600 元（300 千米×2 元/千米）。

3. 人员差旅费：1 100 元（3 人）。

费用共计 2 900 元。

实训任务：

请以福建省××股份有限公司 John 身份给××国际货运代理有限公司 Candy 撰写以上事件的索赔函。

【任务分析】请小组讨论详述索赔事由，并用英文复述。

【任务分析】请小组讨论详述索赔要求，并用英文复述。

【制订方案】请小组讨论根据商务信函三段式法则分别拟出信函的段落大意。

【任务实施】请撰写索赔函。

三、识读投诉函、索赔函

【任务要求】学习以下投诉函、索赔函，并完成相应任务。

From：Guangzhou Huacheng **Agricultural** Products Trading Co.，Ltd

To：American bright Trading Co.，Ltd

Send：July 28，2021

Subject：**Claim for** Short－Weight

Dear Mr. Clare,

Thank you for your **promptness** in shipping the **polished rice** from Los Angeles by OOCL we ordered on July 6, but we find that only 298 tons of the same were delivered **whereas** our order was for 300 tons.

To support our **statement** , we mail one copy of inspection **certification** from Guangzhou **Commodity** inspection **Bureau**. On basis of the inspection certificate, we hereby **lodge** our claim with you for US ＄ 1000 in all.

We are sure that you will give our claims your most favorable **consideration** and we look forward to your **settlement** at an early date.

Your sincerely,

Li Hua

【任务分析】

◆按要求记录重点词汇。

_____

_____

_____

_____

_____

_____

_____

_____

◆Regarding this shipment, fill in the blanks based on above mails.

1. mode of transportation:

2. name of commodity:

3. country of origin:

4. country of destination:

5. port of loading:

6. port of transshipment:

7. carrier:

8. ETD:

9. port of discharge:

10. ETA:

11. shipper on MBL:

12. inspection body:

13. cargo weight:

14. claim amount:

15. subject of the letter:

【任务实施】请翻译信函。

_____

_____

_____

学习任务七（2）索赔函 英文词汇学习

四、索赔函典型句式

Translate the following sentences.

(From Chinese into English or from English into Chinese.)

1. 我们遗憾地通知贵方，运来的货物明显与样品不符。

2. 由于这批货短量，我们要对卖方提出索赔。

_____

_____

3. 盼望你们能早日理赔。

_____

_____

4. 此次索赔的对象应是承运人或保险人，而不是我方。

_____

_____

5. The principle of punctuality should be noticed when a claim is lodged.

_____

_____

6. The chance of getting compensation might be missed if the deadline of a valid claim period is passed.

_____

_____

7. We have to lodge a claim against you on this shipment for ＄200 on account of short weight.

_____

_____

学习活动3　理赔函识读与撰写

学习目标

1. **知识目标**
   - ◆能熟记理赔函的基本词汇。
   - ◆能掌握理赔函的典型句式。
   - ◆能复述理赔函的写作内容。
   - ◆能识读信息分析客户需求。

2. 技能目标

◆能熟练掌握商务信函三段式法则。

◆能识读函电中的特殊用语，根据中心词汇准确把握函电意图。

◆能够根据客户要求，运用英语灵活处理理赔函中的日常业务。

3. 素养目标

◆通过各种学习工具提高自主学习能力，增强英语学习兴趣。

◆通过情景模拟增强对工作岗位的认知感，提高与国际客户沟通交流的信心。

◆通过小组合作增强沟通表达能力，培养团结合作精神，提高工作抗压能力。

学习课时

8 课时

学习过程

一、索赔函与理赔函识读

【工作情境】以下是我们收到的索赔函，请认真阅读。

From：Guangzhou Huacheng Agricultural Products Trading Co.，Ltd

To：Guangzhou Voyage Logistics Co.，Ltd

Send：July 29，2021

Subject：Claim for rotten apple on B/L NO. OOLU562584

Dear Sara，

Here we refer to the container B/L NO. OOLU562584 loaded at our warehouse which we have received a claim letter from our consignee yesterday.

You could check the detail information on the attachment. Our consignee was dissatisfied with this result. We have no choice but to lodge a claim with you for USD 2 000 in all.

We hope that this matter can be resolved as soon as possible.

Yours faithfully，

Candy

Attachment：

From：American Bright Trading Co., Ltd
To：Guangzhou Huacheng Agricultural Products Trading Co., Ltd
Send：July 28, 2021
Subject：Claim for rotten apple
Dear Candy,

We are pleased to inform you that we have received one container of Fuji Apple under S/C NO. YX20211103 （@ CIF price） at our warehouse NO. 1 yesterday.

But we regret to tell you that we find 123 cartons of the apple rotten. These give a damage rate of 9.73%. To support our statement, we have asked the third party inspection **authority** to come here this morning. Enclosed please find the **survey report** and pictures. You can get more information here.

We believe that the above information is clear to you. It had **aterrible effect** on us. Hope you could settle this problem as soon as possible. If you need any other information, please contact us quickly.
Thanks in advance.
Best Regards.
Jack

【任务分析】
◆按要求记录重点词汇。

_____

_____

_____

_____

_____

_____

_____

_____

◆请根据信函内容完成以下关系方的填充。

Consignee	Shipper	Forwarder

_____ received goods from _____ on July 27，2021.

_____ send email to _____ on July 28，2021.

_____ received a claim letter from _____ on July 29，2021.

◆Regarding this shipment，fill in the blanks based on above mails.

1. mode of transportation：

2. name of commodity：

3. country of origin：

4. country of destination：

5. port of loading：

6. port of transshipment：

7. carrier：

8. ETD：

9. port of discharge：

10. ETA：

11. shipper on MBL：

12. forwarder：

13. cartons of rotten apple：

14. claim amount from shipper：

15. subject of the letter：

【任务分析】请阅读以下理赔函，小组讨论根据商务信函三段式法则分别拟出信函的段落大意。

Dear Sirs，

Thank you for your letter of May 20 with a claim for breakages. Your claim is for GB ￡ 200 on the shipment delivered on May 18 to your order No. 2423.

The goods were in perfect order and properly packed in cardboard boxes. They were then placed in **a sealed** container at our factory. It is difficult to imagine how many breakages could occur.

Fortunately, the goods were fully insured under our standard policy with Lloyds of London, but in order to make a claim we shall need much more information. Please make a complete inventory of the broken items and send it to us. We shall then contact our insurer. Their agent will probably call on you to check the consignment.

I apologize for the inconvenience caused.

Best regards,

Kate

_____

_____

_____

_____

_____

学习任务七（3）索赔函理赔函英文词汇学习

二、理赔函撰写

【工作情境】以上是我们收到的索赔函，请认真阅读。

实训任务：

请以广州××物流有限公司的 Sara 身份给广州××农产品贸易有限公司的 Candy 回复其索赔函。

请以广州××农产品贸易有限公司的 Candy 身份给美国××贸易有限公司的 Jack 撰写理赔函。

【任务分析】请小组讨论分析理赔函要素。

_____

_____

【任务分析】请小组讨论分析索赔函处理步骤。

【制订方案】请小组讨论根据商务信函三段式法则分别拟出信函的段落大意。

【任务实施】请撰写理赔函。

附：

商务信函评价标准

项目	细则
商务信函格式	正确采用商务信函全齐头式，信函包含以下主要要素：发件人、收件人、日期、邮件主题及正文
商务信函写作原则	遵循商务信函写作七原则：完整、具体、清楚、简洁、礼貌、体谅、正确
商务信函三段式法则	符合商务信函三段式法则，段落大意清晰明了，承上启下
商务信函典型句式	完整、规范、正确地涵盖该类信函的典型句式和专业术语
综合运用能力	能运用规范的英文灵活处理、解决信息变更函的交流业务

学生优秀样函：

学生优秀样函

参考文献

［1］编写组. 国际货代函电实训教程［M］. 北京：高等教育出版社，2013.

［2］郑晓泉，廖晓燕. 外贸函电实务［M］. 北京：人民邮电出版社，2011.

［3］贾庆. 国际货运代理：海外实务篇（双语版）［M］. 北京：清华大学出版社，2015.

［4］杜海涛. 我国进出口规模首次突破40万亿元［N］. 人民日报，2023-01-14（01）.